The Bondman by Philip Massinger

Philip Massinger was baptized at St. Thomas's in Salisbury on November 24th, 1583.

Massinger is described in his matriculation entry at St. Alban Hall, Oxford (1602), as the son of a gentleman. His father, who had also been educated there, was a member of parliament, and attached to the household of Henry Herbert, 2nd Earl of Pembroke. The Earl was later seen as a potential patron for Massinger.

He left Oxford in 1606 without a degree. His father had died in 1603, and accounts suggest that Massinger was left with no financial support this, together with rumours that he had converted to Catholicism, meant the next stage of his career needed to provide an income.

Massinger went to London to make his living as a dramatist, but he is only recorded as author some fifteen years later, when The Virgin Martyr (1621) is given as the work of Massinger and Thomas Dekker.

During those early years as a playwright he wrote for the Elizabethan stage entrepreneur, Philip Henslowe. It was a difficult existence. Poverty was always close and there was constant pleading for advance payments on forthcoming works merely to survive.

After Henslowe died in 1616 Massinger and John Fletcher began to write primarily for the King's Men and Massinger would write regularly for them until his death.

The tone of the dedications in later plays suggests evidence of his continued poverty. In the preface of The Maid of Honour (1632) he wrote, addressing Sir Francis Foljambe and Sir Thomas Bland: "I had not to this time subsisted, but that I was supported by your frequent courtesies and favours."

The prologue to The Guardian (1633) refers to two unsuccessful plays and two years of silence, when the author feared he had lost popular favour although, from the little evidence that survives, it also seems he had involved some of his plays with political characters which would have cast shadows upon England's alliances.

Philip Massinger died suddenly at his house near the Globe Theatre on March 17th, 1640. He was buried the next day in the churchyard of St. Saviour's, Southwark, on March 18th, 1640. In the entry in the parish register he is described as a "stranger," which, however, implies nothing more than that he belonged to another parish.

Index of Contents

THE HISTORY OF THE PLAY

The Bondman was performed, as we learn from the Office-book of Sir Henry Herbert, Master of the Revels, at the Cockpit in Drury-lane, December 3, 1623. It was printed the following year, and again in 1638.

The main incident of the plot is taken from the life of Timoleon, as related by Plutarch. The revolt and subsequent reduction of the slaves to their duty may have been taken either from Herodotus or Justin, or Purchas's Pilgrim. The artifice by which they are quelled is silly and unnatural, and its introduction degrades a very beautifully managed plot.

The play was revived in 1660 by Betterton, who played Pisander; and several alterations of it have since been produced, but without success.

Our author never writes with more effect than when he combines his own fancy with real history; and in The Bondman he has produced a piece which is, with few exceptions, at once stately and playful, impressive and tender. He matures the love under the cover of the history; till at length the interest changes, and the history becomes subordinate to the love.

The characters are drawn with much variety and interest. The modest gravity and self-command of Timoleon well agrees with the ancient descriptions of the man from whose mouth nihil unquam insolens, neque gloriosum exiit.

RIGHT HONOURABLE,

However I could never arrive at the happiness to be made known to your lordship, yet a desire, born with me, to make a tender of all duties and service to the noble family of the Herberts, descended to me as an inheritance from my dead father, Arthur Massinger. Many years he happily spent in the service of your honourable house, and died a servant to it; leaving his to be ever most glad and ready to be at the command of all such as derive themselves from his most honoured master, your lordship's most noble father. The consideration of this encouraged me (having no other means to present my humblest service to your honour) to shroud this trifle under the wings of your noble protection; and I hope, out of the clemency of your heroic disposition, it will find, though perhaps not a welcome entertainment, yet, at the worst, a gracious pardon. When it was first acted, your lordship's liberal suffrage taught others to allow it for current, it having received the undoubted stamp of your lordship's allowance: and if in the perusal of any vacant hour, when your honour's more serious occasions shall give you leave to read it, it answer, in your lordship's judgment, the report and opinion it had upon the stage, I shall esteem my labours not ill employed, and, while I live, continue

the humblest of those that
truly honour your lordship,
PHILIP MASSINGER.

DRAMATIS PERSONÆ

TIMOLEON, the general, of Corinth.
ARCHIDAMUS, prætor of Syracusa.
DIPHILUS, a senator of Syracusa.
CLEON, a fat foolish lord.
MARULLO, the Bondman (i. e. PISANDER, a gentleman of Thebes, disguised as a slave).
POLIPHRON, friend to MARULLO, also disguised as a slave.
LEOSTHENES, a gentleman of Syracusa, enamoured of CLEORA.
ASOTUS, a foolish lover, and the son of CLEON.
TIMAGORAS, the son of ARCHIDAMUS.
GRACCULO,   } slaves.
CIMBRIO,   }
A Gaoler.

CLEORA, daughter of ARCHIDAMUS.
CORISCA, a proud lady, wife to CLEON.
OLYMPIA, a rich widow.
TIMANDRA, slave to CLEORA (i. e. STATILIA, sister to PISANDER).
ZANTHIA, slave to CORISCA.

Other Slaves, Soldiers, Officers, Senators.

THE BONDMAN.

ACT I

SCENE I

The Camp of Timoleon, near Syracuse

Enter **TIMAGORAS** and **LEOSTHENES**.

TIMAGORAS
Why should you droop, Leosthenes, or despair
My sister's favour? What, before, you purchased
By courtship and fair language, in these wars
(For from her soul you know she loves a soldier)
You may deserve by action.

LEOSTHENES
Good Timagoras,
When I have said my friend, think all is spoken
That may assure me yours; and pray you believe,
The dreadful voice of war that shakes the city,
The thundering threats of Carthage, nor their army
Raised to make good those threats, affright not me.—
If fair Cleora were confirm'd his prize
That has the strongest arm and sharpest sword,
I'd court Bellona in her horrid trim,
As if she were a mistress; and bless fortune,
That offers my young valour to the proof,
How much I dare do for your sister's love.
But, when that I consider how averse
Your noble father, great Archidamus,
Is, and hath ever been, to my desires,
Reason may warrant me to doubt and fear,
What seeds soever I sow in these wars
Of noble courage, his determinate will
May blast, and give my harvest to another,
That never toil'd for it.

TIMAGORAS
Prithee, do not nourish

These jealous thoughts; I am thine, (and pardon me,
Though I repeat it,) thy Timagoras,
That, for thy sake, when the bold Theban sued,
Far-famed Pisander, for my sister's love,
Sent him disgraced and discontented home.
I wrought my father then; and I, that stopp'd not
In the career of my affection to thee,
When that renowned worthy, that brought with him
High birth, wealth, courage, as feed advocates
To mediate for him; never will consent
A fool, that only has the shape of man,
Asotus, though he be rich Cleon's heir,
Shall bear her from thee.

LEOSTHENES
In that trust I love.

TIMAGORAS
Which never shall deceive you.

[Enter **MARULLO**.

MARULLO
Sir, the general,
Timoleon, by his trumpets hath given warning
For a remove.

TIMAGORAS
'Tis well; provide my horse.

MARULLO
I shall, sir.

[Exit.

LEOSTHENES
This slave has a strange aspect.

TIMAGORAS
Fit for his fortune; 'tis a strong-limb'd knave:
My father bought him for my sister's litter.
O pride of women! Coaches are too common—
They surfeit in the happiness of peace,
And ladies think they keep not state enough,
If, for their pomp and ease [1], they are not borne
In triumph on men's shoulders.

LEOSTHENES

Who commands
The Carthaginian fleet?

TIMAGORAS
Gisco's their admiral,
And 'tis our happiness; a raw young fellow,
One never train'd in arms, but rather fashion'd
To tilt with ladies' lips, than crack a lance;
Ravish a feather from a mistress' fan[2],
And wear it as a favour. A steel helmet,
Made horrid with a glorious plume, will crack
His woman's neck.

LEOSTHENES
No more of him.—The motives,
That Corinth gives us aid?

TIMAGORAS
The common danger;
For Sicily being afire, she is not safe:
It being apparent that ambitious Carthage,
That, to enlarge her empire, strives to fasten
An unjust gripe on us that live free lords
Of Syracusa, will not end, till Greece
Acknowledge her their sovereign.

LEOSTHENES
I am satisfied.
What think you of our general?

TIMAGORAS
He's a man   [Trumpets within.
Of strange and reserved parts; but a great soldier.
His trumpets call us, I'll forbear his character:
To-morrow, in the senate-house, at large
He will express himself.

LEOSTHENES
I'll follow you.

[Exeunt.

FOOTNOTES

[1] If, for their pomp and ease, &c.] Mr. Gilchrist thinks (and I believe rightly) that Massinger, who evidently regarded the Duke of Buckingham with no favourable eye, here reflects on the use of sedan-chairs, which his grace first introduced, from Spain, about this period. They were carried, as Massinger

says, "on men's shoulders," and the novelty provoked no small displeasure against the favourite, who, in thus employing his servants, was charged, by the writers of those times, with "degrading Englishmen into slaves and beasts of burden, to gratify his inordinate vanity."—GIFFORD.

[2] Fan.] The fan of our ancestors was not at all in the shape of the implement now used under the same name, but more like a hand-skreen. It had a roundish handle, and was frequently composed of feathers.

SCENE II

Syracuse. The Senate-House.

Enter **ARCHIDAMUS, CLEON, DIPHILUS, OLYMPIA, CORISCA, CLEORA**, and **ZANTHIA**.

ARCHIDAMUS
So careless we have been, my noble lords,
In the disposing of our own affairs,
And ignorant in the art of government,
That now we need a stranger to instruct us.
Yet we are happy that our neighbour Corinth,
Pitying the unjust gripe Carthage would lay
On Syracusa, hath vouchsafed to lend us
Her man of men, Timoleon, to defend
Our country and our liberties.

DIPHILUS
'Tis a favour
We are unworthy of, and we may blush
Necessity compels us to receive it.

ARCHIDAMUS
O shame! that we, that are a populous nation,
Engaged to liberal nature for all blessings
An island can bring forth; we, that have limbs,
And able bodies; shipping, arms, and treasure,
The sinews of the war, now we are call'd
To stand upon our guard, cannot produce
One fit to be our general.

CLEON
I am old and fat;
I could say something, else.

ARCHIDAMUS
We must obey
The time and our occasions; ruinous buildings,
Whose bases and foundations are infirm,

Must use supporters: we are circled round
With danger; o'er our heads, with sail-stretch'd wings,
Destruction hovers, and a cloud of mischief
Ready to break upon us; no hope left us
That may divert it, but our sleeping virtue,
Roused up by brave Timoleon.

CLEON
When arrives he?

DIPHILUS
He is expected every hour.

ARCHIDAMUS
The braveries [1]
Of Syracusa, among whom my son,
Timagoras, Leosthenes, and Asotus,
Your hopeful heir, lord Cleon, two days since
Rode forth to meet him, and attend him to
The city; every minute we expect
To be bless'd with his presence.

[Shouts within; then a flourish of trumpets.

CLEON
What shout's this?

DIPHILUS
'Tis seconded with loud music.

ARCHIDAMUS
Which confirms
His wish'd-for entrance. Let us entertain him
With all respect, solemnity, and pomp,
A man may merit, that comes to redeem us
From slavery and oppression.

CLEON
I'll lock up
My doors, and guard my gold: these lads of Corinth
Have nimble fingers, and I fear them more,
Being within our walls, than those of Carthage;
They are far off.

ARCHIDAMUS
And, ladies, be it your care
To welcome him and his followers with all duty:
For rest resolved, their hands and swords must keep you

In that full height of happiness you live;
A dreadful change else follows.

[Exeunt **ARCHIDAMUS, CLEON,** and **DIPHILUS**.

OLYMPIA
We are instructed.

CORISCA
Musing, Cleora?

OLYMPIA
She's studying how to entertain these strangers,
And to engross them to herself.

CLEORA
No, surely.

OLYMPIA
No more; they come.

[Flourish of trumpets. Enter **TIMAGORAS, LEOSTHENES, ASOTUS, TIMOLEON** in black, led in by
ARCHIDAMUS, DIPHILUS, and **CLEON**; followed by **MARULLO, GRACCULO, CIMBRIO,** and other **SLAVES**.

ARCHIDAMUS
It is your seat: which, with a general suffrage,

[Offering **TIMOLEON** the state [2].

As to the supreme magistrate, Sicily tenders,
And prays Timoleon to accept.

TIMOLEON
Such honours
To one ambitious of rule [3] or titles,
Whose heaven on earth is placed in his command,
And absolute power o'er others, would with joy,
And veins swollen high with pride, be entertain'd.
They take not me; for I have ever loved
An equal freedom, and proclaim'd all such
As would usurp on others' liberties
Rebels to nature, to whose bounteous blessings
All men lay claim as true legitimate sons:
But such as have made forfeit of themselves
By vicious courses, and their birthright lost,
'Tis not injustice they are mark'd for slaves,
To serve the virtuous. For myself, I know
Honours and great employments are great burdens,

And must require an Atlas to support them.
He that would govern others, first should be
The master of himself, richly endued
With depth of understanding, height of courage,
And those remarkable graces which I dare not
Ascribe unto myself.

ARCHIDAMUS
Sir, empty men
Are trumpets of their own deserts; but you,
That are not in opinion, but in proof,
Really good, and full of glorious parts,
Leave the report of what you are to fame,
Which, from the ready tongues of all good men,
Aloud proclaims you.

DIPHILUS
Besides, you stand bound,
Having so large a field to exercise
Your active virtues offer'd you, to impart
Your strength to such as need it.

TIMOLEON
'Tis confess'd;
And, since you'll have it so, such as I am,
For you, and for the liberty of Greece,
I am most ready to lay down my life:
But yet consider, men of Syracusa,
Before that you deliver up the power,
Which yet is yours, to me,—to whom 'tis given;
To an impartial man, with whom nor threats
Nor prayers shall prevail; for I must steer
An even course.

ARCHIDAMUS
Which is desired of all.

TIMOLEON
Timophanes, my brother [4], for whose death
I am tainted in the world, and foully tainted;
In whose remembrance I have ever worn,
In peace and war, this livery of sorrow;
Can witness for me how much I detest
Tyrannous usurpation. With grief
I must remember it; for when no persuasion
Could win him to desist from his bad practice,
To change the aristocracy of Corinth
Into an absolute monarchy, I chose rather

To prove a pious and obedient son
To my country, my best mother [5], than to lend
Assistance to Timophanes, though my brother,
That, like a tyrant, strove to set his foot
Upon the city's freedom.

TIMAGORAS
'Twas a deed
Deserving rather trophies than reproof.

LEOSTHENES
And will be still remember'd to your honour,
If you forsake not us.

DIPHILUS
If you free Sicily
From barbarous Carthage' yoke [6], it will be said
In him you slew a tyrant.

ARCHIDAMUS
But, giving way
To her invasion, not vouchsafing us
That fly to your protection aid and comfort,
'Twill be believed that, for your private ends,
You kill'd a brother.

TIMOLEON
As I then proceed,
To all posterity may that act be crown'd
With a deserved applause, or branded with
The mark of infamy.—Stay yet: ere I take
This seat of justice, or engage myself
To fight for you abroad, or to reform
Your state at home, swear all upon my sword,
And call the gods of Sicily to witness
The oath you take, that whatsoe'er I shall
Propound for safety of your commonwealth,
Not circumscribed or bound in, shall by you
Be willingly obey'd.

ARCHIDAMUS, DIPHILUS, CLEON
So may we prosper,
As we obey in all things!

TIMAGORAS, LEOSTHENES ASOTUS
And observe
All your commands as oracles!

TIMOLEON
Do not repent it.

[Takes the state.

OLYMPIA
He ask'd not our consent.

CORISCA
He's a clown, I warrant him.

OLYMPIA
He thinks women
No part of the republic.

CORISCA
He shall find
We are a commonwealth.

CLEON
The less your honour.

TIMOLEON
First, then, a word or two, but without bitterness,
(And yet mistake me not, I am no flatterer,)
Concerning your ill government of the state;
In which the greatest, noblest, and most rich,
Stand, in the first file, guilty.

CLEON
Ha! how's this?

TIMOLEON
You have not, as good patriots should do, studied
The public good, but your particular ends;
Factious among yourselves, preferring such
To offices and honours, as ne'er read
The elements of saving policy,
But deeply skill'd in all the principles
That usher to destruction.

LEOSTHENES
Sharp!

TIMAGORAS
The better.

TIMOLEON

Your senate-house, which used not to admit
A man, however popular, to stand
At the helm of government, whose youth was not
Made glorious by action; whose experience,
Crown'd with gray hairs, gave warrant to his counsels,
Heard and received with reverence; is now fill'd
With green heads, that determine of the state
Over their cups, or when their sated lusts
Afford them leisure; or supplied by those
Who, rising from base arts and sordid thrift,
Are eminent for their wealth, not for their wisdom:
Which is the reason that to hold a place
In council, which was once esteem'd an honour,
And a reward for virtue, hath quite lost
Lustre and reputation, and is made
A mercenary purchase.

TIMAGORAS
He speaks home.

LEOSTHENES
And to the purpose.

TIMOLEON
From whence it proceeds,
That the treasure of the city is engross'd
By a few private men, the public coffers
Hollow with want; and they, that will not spare
One talent for the common good, to feed
The pride and bravery of their wives, consume,
In plate, in jewels, and superfluous slaves,
What would maintain an army.

CORISCA
Have at us!

OLYMPIA
We thought we were forgot.

CLEON
But it appears
You will be treated of.

TIMOLEON
Yet, in this plenty,
And fat of peace, your young men ne'er were train'd
In martial discipline; and your ships unrigg'd
Rot in the harbour: no defence prepared,

But thought unuseful; as if that the gods,
Indulgent to your sloth, had granted you
A perpetuity of pride and pleasure,
No change fear'd or expected. Now you find
That Carthage, looking on your stupid sleeps
And dull security, was invited to
Invade your territories.

ARCHIDAMUS
You have made us see, sir,
To our shame, the country's sickness: now from you,
As from a careful and a wise physician,
We do expect the cure.

TIMOLEON
Old fester'd sores
Must be lanced to the quick, and cauterized;
Which borne with patience, after I'll apply
Soft unguents. For the maintenance of the war,
It is decreed all moneys in the hand
Of private men shall instantly be brought
To the public treasury.

TIMAGORAS
This bites sore.

CLEON
The cure
Is worse than the disease; I'll never yield to 't:
What could the enemy, though victorious,
Inflict more on us? All that my youth hath toil'd for,
Purchased with industry, and preserved with care,
Forced from me in a moment!

DIPHILUS
This rough course
Will never be allow'd of.

TIMOLEON
O blind men!
If you refuse the first means that is offer'd
To give you health, no hope's left to recover
Your desperate sickness. Do you prize your muck
Above your liberties? and rather choose
To be made bondmen, than to part with that
To which already you are slaves? Or can it
Be probable, in your flattering apprehensions,
You can capitulate with the conquerors,

And keep that yours which they come to possess,
And, while you kneel in vain, will ravish from you?
—But take your own ways; brood upon your gold.
Sacrifice to your idol, and preserve
The prey entire, and merit the report
Of careful stewards: yield a just account
To your proud masters, who, with whips of iron,
Will force you to give up what you conceal,
Or tear it from your throats: adorn your walls
With Persian hangings wrought of gold and pearl;
Cover the floors on which they are to tread
With costly Median silks; perfume the rooms
With cassia and amber, where they are
To feast and revel; while, like servile grooms,
You wait upon their trenchers: feed their eyes
With massy plate, until your cupboards crack
With the weight that they sustain; and, to perfect
Their entertainment, offer up your sons
And able men for slaves; while you, that are
Unfit for labour, are spurn'd out to starve,
Unpitied, in some desert, no friend by,
Whose sorrow may spare one compassionate tear
In the remembrance of what once you were.

LEOSTHENES
The blood turns.

TIMAGORAS
Observe how old Cleon shakes,
As if in picture he had shown him what
He was to suffer.

CORISCA
I am sick: the man
Speaks poniards and diseases.

OLYMPIA
O my doctor!
I never shall recover.

CLEON [coming forward]
If a virgin,
Whose speech was ever yet usher'd with fear,
One knowing modesty and humble silence
To be the choicest ornaments of our sex,
In the presence of so many reverend men
Struck dumb with terror and astonishment,
Presume to clothe her thought in vocal sounds,

Let her find pardon. First to you, great sir,
A bashful maid's thanks, and her zealous prayers
Wing'd with pure innocence, bearing them to heaven,
For all prosperity that the gods can give
To one whose piety must exact their care,
Thus low I offer.

TIMOLEON
'Tis a happy omen.
Rise, blest one, and speak boldly. On my virtue,
I am thy warrant from so clear a spring
Sweet rivers ever flow.

CLEON
Then, thus to you,
My noble father, and these lords, to whom
I next owe duty: no respect forgotten
To you, my brother, and these bold young men,
(Such I would have them,) that are, or should he,
The city's sword and target of defence.
To all of you I speak; and, if a blush
Steal on my cheeks, it is shown to reprove
Your paleness, willingly I would not say,
Your cowardice or fear: Think you all treasure
Hid in the bowels of the earth, or shipwreck'd
In Neptune's wat'ry kingdom, can hold weight,
When liberty and honour fill one scale,
Triumphant Justice sitting on the beam?
Or dare you but imagine that your gold is
Too dear a salary for such as hazard
Their blood and lives in your defence? For me,
An ignorant girl, bear witness, heaven! so far
I prize a soldier, that, to give him pay,
With such devotion as our flamens offer
Their sacrifices at the holy altar,
I do lay down these jewels, will make sale
Of my superfluous wardrobe, to supply
The meanest of their wants.

[Lays down her jewels, &c.; the rest follow her example.

TIMOLEON
Brave masculine spirit!

DIPHILUS
We are shown, to our shame, what we in honour
Should have taught others.

ARCHIDAMUS
Such a fair example
Must needs be follow'd.

TIMAGORAS
Ever my dear sister,
But now our family's glory!

LEOSTHENES
Were she deform'd,
The virtues of her mind would force a stoic
To sue to be her servant.

CLEON
I must yield;
And, though my heart-blood part with it, I will
Deliver in my wealth.

ASOTUS
I would say something;
But, the truth is, I know not what.

TIMOLEON
We have money;
And men must now be thought on.

ARCHIDAMUS
We can press
Of labourers in the country, men inured
To cold and heat, ten thousand.

DIPHILUS
Or, if need be,
Enrol our slaves, lusty and able varlets,
And fit for service.

CLEON
They shall go for me;
I will not pay and fight too.

CLEON
How! your slaves?
O stain of honour!—Once more, sir, your pardon;
And, to their shames, let me deliver what
I know in justice you may speak.

TIMOLEON
Most gladly:

I could not wish my thoughts a better organ
Than your tongue, to express them.

CLEON
Are you men!
(For age may qualify, though not excuse,
The backwardness of these,) able young men!
Yet, now your country's liberty's at the stake,
Honour and glorious triumph made the garland
For such as dare deserve them; a rich feast
Prepared by Victory, of immortal viands,
Not for base men, but such as with their swords
Dare force admittance, and will be her guests:
And can you coldly suffer such rewards
To be proposed to labourers and slaves?
While you, that are born noble, to whom these,
Valued at their best rate, are next to horses,
Or other beasts of carriage, cry aim [7]!
Like idle lookers on, till their proud worth
Make them become your masters!

TIMOLEON
By my hopes,
There's fire and spirit enough in this to make
Thersites valiant.

CLEON
No; far, far be it from you:
Let these of meaner quality contend
Who can endure most labour; plough the earth,
And think they are rewarded when their toil
Brings home a fruitful harvest to their lords;
Let them prove good artificers, and serve you
For use and ornament, but not presume
To touch at what is noble. If you think them
Unworthy to taste of those cates you feed on,
Or wear such costly garments, will you grant them
The privilege and prerogative of great minds,
Which you were born to? Honour won in war,
And to be styled preservers of their country,
Are titles fit for free and generous spirits,
And not for bondmen. Had I been born a man,
And such ne'er-dying glories made the prize
To bold heroic courage, by Diana,
I would not to my brother, nay, my father,
Be bribed to part with the least piece of honour
I should gain in this action!

TIMOLEON
She's inspired,
Or in her speaks the genius of your country,
To fire your blood in her defence: I am rapt
With the imagination. Noble maid,
Timoleon is your soldier, and will sweat
Drops of his best blood, but he will bring home
Triumphant conquest to you. Let me wear
Your colours, lady; and though youthful heats,
That look no further than your outward form,
Are long since buried in me; while I live,
I am a constant lover of your mind,
That does transcend all precedents.

CLEON
'Tis an honour,

[Gives her scarf.

And so I do receive it.

LEOSTHENES
I am for the journey.

TIMAGORAS
May all diseases sloth and luxury bring
Fall upon him that stays at home!

ARCHIDAMUS
Though old,
I will be there in person.

DIPHILUS
So will I:
Methinks I am not what I was; her words
Have made me younger, by a score of years,
Than I was when I came hither.

CLEON
I shall never
Make a good soldier, and therefore desire
To be excused at home.

ASOTUS
'Tis my suit too.

TIMOLEON
Have your desires; you would be burthens to us.—

Lead, fairest, to the temple; first we'll pay
A sacrifice to the gods for good success:
For all great actions the wish'd course do run,
That are, with their allowance, well begun.

[Exeunt all but, **MARULLO, GRACCULO** and **CIMBRIO**.

MARULLO
Stay, Cimbrio and Gracculo.

CIMBRIO
The business?

MARULLO
Meet me to-morrow night near to the grove,
Neighbouring the east part of the city.

GRACCULO
Well.

MARULLO
And bring the rest of our condition with you:
I've something to impart may break our fetters,
If you dare second me.

CIMBRIO
We'll not fail.

GRACCULO
A cart-rope
Shall not bind me at home.

MARULLO
Think on 't, and prosper.

[Exeunt.

FOOTNOTES:

[1] The braveries,] i. e. the gay and fashionable gallants of the town.

[2] The state.] This was a raised platform, on which was placed a chair with a canopy over it. The word occurs perpetually in our old writers. It is used by Dryden, but seems to have been growing obsolete while he was writing: in the first edition of Mac Fleckno, the monarch is placed on a state; in the subsequent ones, he is seated like his fellow kings, on a throne: it occurs also, and I believe for the last time, in Swift: "As she affected not the grandeur of a state with a canopy, she thought there was no offence in an elbow chair."—Hist. of John Bull, c.i.—GIFFORD.

[3] *—Such honours*
To one ambitious of rule, &c.] Massinger has here finely drawn the character of Timoleon, and been very
true to history. He was descended from one of the noblest families in Corinth, loved his country
passionately, and discovered upon all occasions a singular humanity of temper, except against tyrants
and bad men. He was an excellent captain; and as in his youth he had all the maturity of age, in age he
had all the fire and courage of the most ardent youth.—COXETER.

[4] *Timol. Timophanes, my brother, &c.] Timoleon had an elder brother, called Timophanes, whom he*
tenderly loved, as he had demonstrated in a battle, in which he covered him with his body, and saved his
life at the great danger of his own. But his country was still dearer to him. That brother having made
himself tyrant of it, so black a crime gave him the sharpest affliction. He made use of all possible means
to bring him back to his duty: kindness, friendship, affection, remonstrances, and even menaces. But
finding all his endeavours ineffectual, and that nothing could prevail upon a heart abandoned to
ambition he caused his brother to be assassinated by two of his friends and intimates, and thought that
upon such an occasion the laws of nature ought to give place to those of his country.—COXETER.

[5] *To my country, my best mother.] In this expression Timoleon alludes to the conduct of his natural*
mother, who would never see him after the assassination of his brother, and always, as Cornelius Nepos
informs us, called him fratricidam, impiumque.—GIFFORD.

[6] *Diph. If you free Sicily From barbarous Carthage' yoke, &c.] This speech and the next are literally from*
Plutarch. Massinger has in this instance adhered more closely to his story than usual.—GIFFORD.

[7] *Cry aim!] i. e. encourage them, as the bystanders do those who are about to shoot at a trial of skill in*
archery.

ACT II

SCENE I

The Same. A Room in Archidamus' House.

Enter **ARCHIDAMUS, TIMAGORAS, LEOSTHENES**, with gorgets; and **MARULLO**.

ARCHIDAMUS
So, so, 'tis well: how do I look?

MARULLO
Most sprightfully.

ARCHIDAMUS
I shrink not in the shoulders; though I'm old
I'm tough, steel to the back; I have not wasted
My stock of strength in featherbeds: here's an arm too;
There's stuff in 't, and I hope will use a sword

As well as any beardless boy of you all.

TIMAGORAS
I'm glad to see you, sir, so well prepared
To endure the travail of the war.

ARCHIDAMUS
Go to, sirrah!
I shall endure, when some of you keep your cabins,
For all your flaunting feathers; nay, Leosthenes,
You are welcome too [1], all friends and fellows now.

LEOSTHENES
Your servant, sir.

ARCHIDAMUS
Pish! leave these compliments,
They stink in a soldier's mouth; I could be merry,
For, now my gown's off, farewell gravity [2]!
I fear ye, when you come to the test.—Old stories tell us,
There's a month call'd October [3], which brings in
Cold weather; there are trenches too, 'tis rumour'd,
In which to stand all night to the knees in water,
In gallants breeds the toothach; there's a sport too,
Named lying perdue, do you mark me? 'tis a game
Which you must learn to play at: now in these seasons,
And choice variety of exercises,
(Nay, I come to you,) and fasts, not for devotion,
Your rambling youngster feels strange alterations;
And in a frosty morning.—O welcome! welcome!

[Enter **DIPHILUS** and **CLEORA**.

You have cut off my discourse; but I will perfect
My lecture in the camp.

DIPHILUS
Come, we are stay'd for;
The general's afire for a remove,
And longs to be in action.

ARCHIDAMUS
'Tis my wish too.
We must part—nay, no tears, my best Cleora;
I shall melt too, and that were ominous.
Millions of blessings on thee! All that's mine
I give up to thy charge; and, sirrah, look
[To **MARULLO.**

You with that care and reverence observe her,
Which you would pay to me.—A kiss; farewell, girl!

DIPHILUS
Peace wait upon you, fair one!

[Exeunt **ARCHIDAMUS**, **DIPHILUS**, and **MARULLO**.

TIMAGORAS
'Twere impertinence
To wish you to be careful of your honour,
That ever keep in pay a guard about you
Of faithful virtues: farewell!—Friend, I leave you
To wipe our kisses off; I know that lovers
Part with more circumstance and ceremony:
Which I give way to.

[Exit.

LEOSTHENES
'Tis a noble favour,
For which I ever owe you. We are alone;
But how I should begin, or in what language
Speak the unwilling word of parting from you,
I am yet to learn.

CLEON
And still continue ignorant;
For I must be most cruel to myself,
If I should teach you.

LEOSTHENES
Yet it must be spoken,
Or you will chide my slackness. You have fired me
With the heat of noble action to deserve you;
And the least spark of honour that took life
From your sweet breath, still fann'd by it and cherish'd,
Must mount up in a glorious flame, or I
Am much unworthy.

CLEON
May it not burn here [4],
And, as a seamark, serve to guide true lovers
Safe from the rocks of passion to the harbour
Of pure affection? rising up an example
Which aftertimes shall witness, to our glory,
First took from us beginning.

LEOSTHENES
'Tis a happiness
My duty to my country, and mine honour
Cannot consent to; besides, add to these,
It was your pleasure, fortified by persuasion,
And strength of reason, for the general good,
That I should go.

CLEON
Alas! I then was witty
To plead against myself; and mine eye, fix'd
Upon the hill of honour, ne'er descended
To look into the vale of certain dangers,
Through which you were to cut your passage to it.

LEOSTHENES
I'll stay at home, then.

CLEON
No, that must not be;
For so, to serve my own ends, and to gain
A petty wreath myself, I rob you of
A certain triumph, which must fall upon you,
Or Virtue's turn'd a handmaid to blind Fortune.
How is my soul divided! to confirm you
In the opinion of the world, most worthy
To be beloved, (with me you're at the height,
And can advance no further,) I must send you
To court the goddess of stern war, who, if
She see you with my eyes, will ne'er return you,
But grow enamour'd of you.

LEOSTHENES
Sweet, take comfort!
And what I offer you, you must vouchsafe me,
Or I am wretched. All the dangers that
I can encounter in the war are trifles;
My enemies abroad to be contemn'd:
The dreadful foes, that have the power to hurt me,
I leave at home with you.

CLEON
With me!

LEOSTHENES
Nay, in you,
In every part about you, they are arm'd
To fight against me.

CLEON
Where?

LEOSTHENES
There's no perfection
That you are mistress of, but musters up
A legion against me, and all sworn
To my destruction.

CLEON
This is strange!

LEOSTHENES
But true, sweet;
Excess of love can work such miracles!
Upon this ivory forehead are intrench'd
Ten thousand rivals, and these suns command
Supplies from all the world, on pain to forfeit
Their comfortable beams; these ruby lips,
A rich exchequer to assure their pay:
This hand, Sibylla's golden bough to guard them
Through hell, and horror, to the Elysian springs;
Which who'll not venture for? and, should I name
Such as the virtues of your mind invite,
Their numbers would be infinite.

CLEON
Can you think
I may be tempted?

LEOSTHENES
You were never proved [5].
For me, I have conversed with you no further
Than would become a brother. I ne'er tuned
Loose notes to your chaste ears; or brought rich presents
For my artillery, to batter down
The fortress of your honour; I never practised
The cunning and corrupting arts they study,
That wander in the wild maze of desire;
Honest simplicity and truth were all
The agents I employ'd; and when I came
To see you, it was with that reverence
As I beheld the altars of the gods:
And Love, that came along with me, was taught
To leave his arrows and his torch behind,
Quench'd in my fear to give offence.

CLEON

And 'twas
That modesty that took me, and preserves me,
Like a fresh rose, in mine own natural sweetness;
Which, sullied with the touch of impure hands,
Loses both scent and beauty.

LEOSTHENES

But, Cleora,
When I am absent, as I must go from you,
(Such is the cruelty of my fate,) and leave you,
Unguarded, to the violent assaults
Of loose temptations; when the memory
Of my so many years of love and service
Is lost in other objects; when you are courted
By such as keep a catalogue of their conquests,
Won upon credulous virgins; when nor father
Is here to owe [6] you, brother to advise you,
Nor your poor servant by, to keep such off,
By love instructed how to undermine,
And blow your constancy up; when your weak senses,
At once assaulted, shall conspire against you,
And play the traitors to your soul, your virtue;
How can you stand? 'Faith, though you fall, and I
The judge, before whom you then stood accused,
I should acquit you.

CLEON

Will you then confirm
That love and jealousy, though of different natures,
Must of necessity be twins; the younger
Created only to defeat the elder,
And spoil him of his birthright [7]? 'tis not well.
But being to part, I will not chide, I will not;
Nor with one syllable or tear, express
How deeply I am wounded with the arrows
Of your distrust: but when that you shall hear,
At your return, how I have borne myself,
And what an austere penance I take on me,
To satisfy your doubts; when, like a vestal,
I show you, to your shame, the fire still burning,
Committed to my charge by true affection,
The people joining with you in the wonder;
When, by the glorious splendour of my sufferings,
The prying eyes of jealousy are struck blind,
The monster too that feeds on fears e'en starved
For want of seeming matter to accuse me;
Expect, Leosthenes, a sharp reproof

From my just anger.

LEOSTHENES
What will you do?

CLEON
Obey me,
Or from this minute you are a stranger to me;
And do 't without reply. All-seeing sun,
Thou witness of my innocence, thus I close
Mine eyes against thy comfortable light,
'Till the return of this distrustful man!
Now bind them sure;—nay, do 't: [He binds her
eyes with her scarf.] If, uncompell'd,
I loose this knot, until the hands that made it
Be pleased to untie it, may consuming plagues
Fall heavy on me! pray you guide me to your lips.
This kiss, when you come back, shall be a virgin
To bid you welcome; nay, I have not done yet:
I will continue dumb, and, you once gone,
No accent shall come from me. Now to my chamber,
My tomb, if you miscarry: there I'll spend
My hours in silent mourning, and thus much
Shall be reported of me to my glory,
And you confess it, whether I live or die,
My constancy triumphs o'er your jealousy.

[Exeunt.

FOOTNOTES:

[1] —nay, Leosthenes,
You are welcome too, &c.] It should be remembered that Archidamus is, with great judgment,
represented in the first scene as averse to the marriage of Leosthenes with his daughter.—GIFFORD.

[2] For, now my gown's off, farewell gravity!] This is said to have been a frequent expression with the
great but playful Sir Thomas More, who was never so happy as when he shook off the pomp of office.
Fuller tells a similar story of Lord Burleigh.—GIFFORD.

[3] There's a month call'd October, &c.] This pleasant old man forgets that he is talking of Sicily, where
October is the most delightful month of the year. All our old poets loved and thought only of their
country. Whatever region was the subject, England was the real theme: their habits, customs,
peculiarities were all derived from thence. This, though it must condemn them as historians, may save
them as patriots: and, indeed, it is not much to be regretted that they should overlook manners, with
which they were very imperfectly acquainted, in favour of those with which they were hourly
conversant—at least it would be ungrateful in us, who profit so much by their minute descriptions, to be
offended at their disregard of "the proper costumi."—GIFFORD.

[4] Here,] i. e. in Syracuse.

[5] Leost. You were never proved.] The whole of this scene is eminently beautiful; yet I cannot avoid recommending to the reader's particular notice the speech which follows. Its rhythm is so perfect, that it drops on the ear like the sweetest melody.—GIFFORD.

[6] Owe,] i. e. own.

[7] And spoil him of his birthright?] This is a happy allusion to the history of Jacob and Esau. It is the more so, for being void of all profaneness; to which, indeed, Massinger had no tendency.—GIFFORD.

SCENE II

The Same. A Room in Cleon's House.

Enter **ASOTUS**, driving in **GRACCULO**.

ASOTUS
You slave! you dog! down, cur!

GRACCULO
Hold, good young master,
For pity's sake!

ASOTUS
Now am I in my kingdom:—
Who says I am not valiant? I begin
To frown again: quake, villain!

GRACCULO
So I do, sir;
Your looks are agues to me.

ASOTUS
Are they so, sir!
'Slight, if I had them at this bay that flout me,
And say I look like a sheep and an ass, I'd make them
Feel that I am a lion.

GRACCULO
Do not roar, sir,
As you are a valiant beast: but do you know
Why you use me thus?

ASOTUS

I'll beat thee a little more,
Then study for a reason. O! I have it:
One brake a jest on me, and then I swore,
(Because I durst not strike him,) when I came home,
That I would break thy head.

GRACCULO
Plague on his mirth!
I am sure I mourn for 't.

ASOTUS
Remember too, I charge you,
To teach my horse good manners yet; this morning,
As I rode to take the air, the untutor'd jade
Threw me, and kick'd me.

GRACCULO
I thank him for 't. [Aside.

ASOTUS
What's that?

GRACCULO
I say, sir, I will teach him to hold his heels,
If you will rule your fingers.

ASOTUS
I'll think upon 't.

GRACCULO
I am bruised to jelly: better be a dog,
Than slave to a fool or coward. [Aside.

ASOTUS
Here's my mother,

[Enter **CORISCA** and **ZANTHIA**.

She is chastising too: how brave we live,
That have our slaves to beat, to keep us in breath
When we want exercise!

CORISCA
Careless creature,

[Striking her.

Look to 't; if a curl fall, or wind or sun

Take my complexion off, I will not leave
One hair upon thine head.

GRACCULO
Here's a second show
Of the family of pride! [Aside.

CORISCA
Fie on these wars!
I'm starved for want of action. When were you with
Your mistress, fair Cleora?

ASOTUS
Two days sithence;
But she's so coy, forsooth, that ere I can
Speak a penn'd speech I have bought and studied for her,
Her woman calls her away.

CORISCA
Here's a dull thing!

ZANTHIA
Madam, my lord.

[Enter **CLEON**.

CLEON
Where are you, wife? I fain would go abroad,
But cannot find my slaves that bear my litter;
I am tired. Your shoulder, son;—nay, sweet, thy hand too:
A turn or two in the garden, and then to supper,
And so to bed.

ASOTUS
Never to rise, I hope, more. [Aside.

[Exeunt.

SCENE III

A Grove near the Walls of Syracuse.

Enter **MARULLO** and **POLIPHRON**. A Table set out with Wine, &c.

MARULLO
'Twill take, I warrant thee.

POLIPHRON
You may do your pleasure;
But, in my judgment, better to make use of
The present opportunity.

MARULLO
No more.

POLIPHRON
I am silenced.

MARULLO
More wine; prithee drink hard, friend,
And when we're hot, whatever I propound,

[Enter **CIMBRIO, GRACCULO**, and other **SLAVES**.

Second with vehemence.—Men of your words, all welcome!
Slaves use no ceremony; sit down; here's a health.

POLIPHRON
Let it run round; fill every man his glass.

GRACCULO
We look for no waiters;—this is wine!

MARULLO
The better,
Strong, lusty wine: drink deep; this juice will make us
As free as our lords.

[Drinks.

GRACCULO
But if they find we taste it,
We are condemn'd to the quarry during life,
Without hope of redemption.

MARULLO
Pish! for that
We'll talk anon: another rouse [1]! we lose time;

[Drinks.

When our low blood's wound up a little higher,
I'll offer my design; nay, we are cold yet;
These glasses contain nothing:—do me right,

[Takes the bottle.

As e'er you hope for liberty. 'Tis done bravely:
How do you feel yourselves now?

CIMBRIO
I begin
To have strange conundrums in my head.

GRACCULO
And I
To loathe base water. I would be hang'd in peace now
For one month of such holidays.

MARULLO
An age, boys,
And yet defy the whip; if you are men,
Or dare believe you have souls.

CIMBRIO
We are no brokers.

MARULLO
Our lords are no gods—

GRACCULO
They are devils to us, I am sure.

MARULLO
But subject to
Cold, hunger, and diseases.

GRACCULO
In abundance.

MARULLO
Equal Nature fashion'd us
All in one mould. The bear serves not the bear,
Nor the wolf the wolf; 'twas odds of strength in tyrants
That pluck'd the first link from the golden chain
With which that THING OF THINGS [2] bound in the world.
Why then, since we are taught, by their examples,
To love our liberty, if not command,
Should the strong serve the weak, the fair, deform'd ones?
Or such as know the cause of things pay tribute
To ignorant fools? All's but the outward gloss,
And politic form, that does distinguish us.—

Cimbrio, thou art a strong man; if, in place
Of carrying burthens, thou hadst been train'd up
In martial discipline, thou might'st have proved
A general, fit to lead and fight for Sicily,
As fortunate as Timoleon.

CIMBRIO
A little fighting
Will serve a general's turn.

MARULLO
Thou, Gracculo,
Hast fluency of language, quick conceit;
And, I think, cover'd with a senator's robe,
Formally set on the bench, thou wouldst appear
As brave a senator.

GRACCULO
Would I had lands,
Or money to buy a place! and if I did not
Sleep on the bench with the drowsiest of them,
Play with my chain, look on my watch, and wear
A state beard, with my barber's help, rank with them
In their most choice peculiar gifts, degrade me,
And put me to drink water again, which, now
I have tasted wine, were poison!

MARULLO
'Tis spoke nobly,
And like a gownman: none of these, I think too,
But would prove good burghers.

GRACCULO
Hum! the fools are modest;
I know their insides: here's an ill-faced fellow,
(But that will not be seen in a dark shop;)
If he did not in a month learn to outswear,
In the selling of his wares, the cunning'st tradesman
In Syracuse, I have no skill. Here's another;
Observe but what a cozening look he has!—
Hold up thy head, man! If, for drawing gallants
Into mortgages for commodities [3], cheating heirs
With your new counterfeit gold thread, and gumm'd velvets,
He does not transcend all that went before him,
Call in his patent.

MARULLO
Is 't not pity, then,

Men of such eminent virtues should be slaves?

CIMBRIO
Our fortune.

MARULLO
'Tis your folly: daring men
Command and make their fates. Say, at this instant,
I mark'd you out a way to liberty;
Possess'd you of those blessings our proud lords
So long have surfeited in; and, what is sweetest,
Arm you with power, by strong hand to revenge
Your stripes, your unregarded toil, the pride,
The insolence, of such as tread upon
Your patient sufferings; fill your famish'd mouths
With the fat and plenty of the land; redeem you
From the dark vale of servitude, and seat you
Upon a hill of happiness; what would you do
To purchase this, and more?

GRACCULO
Do! any thing:
To burn a church or two, and dance by the light on 't,
Were but a May-game.

POLIPHRON
I have a father living;
But if the cutting of his throat could work this,
He should excuse me.

CIMBRIO
'Slight! I would cut mine own,
Rather than miss it; so I might but have
A taste on 't ere I die.

MARULLO
Be resolute men;
You shall run no such hazard, nor groan under
The burden of such crying sins.

POLIPHRON
Do not torment us
With expectation.

MARULLO
Thus, then:—Our proud masters,
And all the able freemen of the city,
Are gone unto the wars—

POLIPHRON

Observe but that.

MARULLO

Old men, and such as can make no resistance,
Are only left at home—

GRACCULO

And the proud young fool,
My master—if this take, I'll hamper him.

MARULLO

Their arsenal, their treasure, 's in our power,
If we have hearts to seize them. If our lords fall
In the present action, the whole country's ours:
Say they return victorious, we have means
To keep the town against them; at the worst,
To make our own conditions. If you dare break up
Their iron chests, banquet in their rich halls,
And carve yourselves of all delights and pleasures
You have been barr'd from, with one voice cry with me,
Liberty! liberty!

OMNES

Liberty! liberty!

MARULLO

Go, then, and take possession: use all freedom;
But shed no blood.

[Exeunt **SLAVES.**]

—So, this is well begun;
But not to be commended till 't be done.

[Exit.

FOOTNOTES:

[1] Rouse,] i. e. full glass, bumper.

[2] That THING OF THINGS.] A literal translation, as Mr. M. Mason observes, of ENS ENTIUM. I know not where Pisander acquired his revolutionary philosophy: his golden chain, perhaps, he found in Homer.—GIFFORD.

ACT III

SCENE I

The Same. A Gallery in Archidamus's House.

Enter **MARULLO** and **TIMANDRA**.

MARULLO
Why, think you that I plot against myself [1]?
Fear nothing, you are safe: these thick-skinn'd slaves,
I use as instruments to serve my ends,
Pierce not my deep designs; nor shall they dare
To lift an arm against you.

TIMANDRA
With your will.
But turbulent spirits, raised beyond themselves
With ease, are not so soon laid; they oft prove
Dangerous to him that call'd them up.

MARULLO
'Tis true,
In what is rashly undertook. Long since
I have consider'd seriously their natures,
Proceeded with mature advice, and know
I hold their will and faculties in more awe
Than I can do my own. Now, for their licence,
And riot in the city, I can make
A just defence and use: it may appear, too,
A politic prevention of such ills
As might, with greater violence and danger,
Hereafter be attempted; though some smart for 't,
It matters not:—however, I'm resolved;
And sleep you with security. Holds Cleora
Constant to her rash vow?

TIMANDRA
Beyond belief;
To me, that see her hourly, it seems a fable.
By signs I guess at her commands, and serve them
With silence; such her pleasure is, made known
By holding her fair hand thus. She eats little,
Sleeps less, as I imagine; once a day
I lead her to this gallery, where she walks
Some half a dozen turns, and, having offer'd
To her absent saint a sacrifice of sighs,
She points back to her prison.

MARULLO
Guide her hither,
And make her understand the slaves' revolt;
And, with your utmost eloquence, enlarge
Their insolence, and wrongs done in the city.
Forget not, too, I am their chief, and tell her
You strongly think my extreme dotage on her,
As I'm Marullo, caused this sudden uproar,
To gain possession of her.

TIMANDRA
Punctually
I will discharge my part.

[Exit.

[Enter **POLIPHRON**.

POLIPHRON
O, sir, I sought you:
There's such variety of all disorders
Among the slaves; answer'd with crying, howling,
By the citizens and their wives; such a confusion,
In a word, not to tire you, as I think
The like was never read of.

MARULLO
This is some
Revenge for my disgrace.

POLIPHRON
But, sir, I fear,
If your authority restrain them not,
They'll fire the city, or kill one another,
They are so apt to outrage; neither know I

Whether you wish it, and came therefore to
Acquaint you with so much.

MARULLO
I will among them;
But must not long be absent.

POLIPHRON
At your pleasure.

[Exeunt.

FOOTNOTE:

[1] Mar. Why, think you that I plot against myself?] The plot opens here with wonderful address; and the succeeding conference, or rather scene, between Pisander and Cleora, is inimitably beautiful.—GIFFORD.

SCENE II

The Same. A Room in the Same.

Shouts within. Enter **CLEORA** and **TIMANDRA**.

TIMANDRA
They are at our gates: my heart! affrights and horrors
Increase each minute. No way left to save us,
No flattering hope to comfort us, or means,
But miracle, to redeem us from base wrongs
And lawless rapine! Are there gods, yet suffer
Such innocent sweetness to be made the spoil
Of brutish violence? And, of these rebel slaves,
He that should offer up his life to guard you,
Marullo, cursed Marullo, your own bondman,
Purchased to serve you, and fed by your favours—
Nay, start not: it is he; he, the grand captain
Of these libidinous beasts, that have not left
One cruel act undone that barbarous conquest
Yet ever practised in a captive city;
He, doting on your beauty, and to have fellows
In his foul sin, hath raised these mutinous slaves.
Wring not your hands, 'tis bootless; use the means
That may preserve you. 'Tis no crime to break
A vow when you are forced to it; show your face,
And with the majesty of commanding beauty
Strike dead his loose affections: if that fail,

Give liberty to your tongue, and use entreaties:
There cannot be a breast of flesh and blood,
Or heart so made of flint, but must receive
Impression from your words; or eyes so stern,
But, from the clear reflection of your tears,
Must melt, and bear them company. Will you not
Do these good offices to yourself? poor I, then,
Can only weep your fortune.—Here he comes.

[Enter **MARULLO**, speaking at the door.

MARULLO
He that advances
A foot beyond this comes upon my sword:
You have had your ways, disturb not mine.

TIMANDRA
Speak gently;
Her fears may kill her else.

MARULLO
Now Love inspire me!
Still shall this canopy of envious night
Obscure my suns of comfort? and those dainties
Of purest white and red, which I take in at
My greedy eyes, denied my famish'd senses?—
The organs of your hearing yet are open;
And you infringe no vow, though you vouchsafe
To give them warrant to convey unto
Your understanding parts the story of
A tortured and despairing lover, whom
Not fortune but affection marks your slave:—
Shake not, best lady! for, believe 't, you are
As far from danger as I am from force:
All violence I shall offer tends no further
Than to relate my sufferings, which I dare not
Presume to do, till, by some gracious sign,
You show you are pleased to hear me.

TIMANDRA
If you are,
Hold forth your right hand.

[**CLEORA** holds forth her right hand.

MARULLO
So, 'tis done; and I
With my glad lips seal humbly on your robe

My soul's thanks for the favour: I forbear
To tell you who I am, what wealth, what honours
I made exchange of, to become your servant:
And though I knew worthy Leosthenes
(For sure he must be worthy, for whose love
You have endured so much) to be my rival,
When rage and jealousy counsell'd me to kill him,
Which then I could have done with much more ease,
Than now, in fear to grieve you, I dare speak it,
Love, seconded with duty, boldly told me
The man I hated, fair Cleora favour'd;
And that was his protection.

[**CLEORA** bows.

TIMANDRA
See, she bows
Her head in sign of thankfulness.

MARULLO
He removed by
The occasion of the war, (my fires increasing
By being closed and stopp'd up,) frantic affection
Prompted me to do something in his absence
That might deliver you into my power,
Which you see is effected: and even now,
When my rebellious passions chide my dulness,
And tell me how much I abuse my fortunes,
Now it is in my power to bear you hence,

[**CLEORA** starts.

(Nay, fear not, madam; true love is a servant,
But brutish lust a tyrant,) only thus much
Be pleased I may speak in my own dear cause;
And think it worthy your consideration,
(I have loved truly, cannot say deserved,
Since duty must not take the name of merit,)
That I so far prize your content, before
All blessings that my hope can fashion to me,
That willingly I entertain despair,
And, for your sake, embrace it; for I know,
This opportunity lost, by no endeavour
The like can be recover'd. To conclude,
Forget not that I lose myself to save you:
For what can I expect but death and torture,
The war being ended? and, what is a task
Would trouble Hercules to undertake,

I do deny you to myself, to give you,
A pure unspotted present, to my rival.
I have said: if it distaste not, best of virgins!
Reward my temperance with some lawful favour,
Though you contemn my person.

[**CLEORA** kneels, then pulls off her glove, and offers her hand to **MARULLO**.

TIMANDRA
See, she kneels,
And seems to call upon the gods to pay
The debt she owes your virtue: to perform which,
As a sure pledge of friendship, she vouchsafes you
Her fair right hand.

MARULLO
I am paid for all my sufferings.
Now, when you please, pass to your private chamber:
My love and duty, faithful guards, shall keep you
From all disturbance; and when you are sated
With thinking of Leosthenes, as a fee
Due to my service, spare one sigh for me.

[Exeunt. **CLEORA** makes a low courtesy as she goes off.

SCENE III

The Same. A Room in Cleon's House.

Enter **GRACCULO**, leading **ASOTUS** in an ape's habit, with a chain about his neck; **ZANTHIA** in CORISCA's clothes, she bearing up her train.

GRACCULO
Come on, sir.

ASOTUS
Oh!

GRACCULO
Do you grumble? you were ever
A brainless ass; but if this hold, I'll teach you
To come aloft and do tricks like an ape.
Your morning's lesson: if you miss—

ASOTUS
O no, sir.

GRACCULO
What for the Carthaginians?

[**ASOTUS** makes mopes [1].]

A good beast.
What for ourself, your lord [2]?

[Dances.]

Exceeding well.
There's your reward.

[Gives him an apple.]

—Not kiss your paw! So, so, so.

ZANTHIA
Was ever lady, the first day of her honour,
So waited on by a wrinkled crone? She looks now,
Without her painting, curling, and perfumes,
Like the last day of January. Further off!
So—stand there like an image; if you stir,
Till, with a quarter of a look, I call you,
You know what follows.

CORISCA
O, what am I fallen to!
But 'tis a punishment for my cruel pride,
Justly return'd upon me.

GRACCULO
How dost thou like
Thy ladyship, Zanthia?

ZANTHIA
Very well; and bear it
With as much state as your lordship.

GRACCULO
Give me thy hand:
Let us, like conquering Romans, walk in triumph [3],
Our captives following; then mount our tribunals,
And make the slaves our footstools.

ZANTHIA
Fine, by Jove!

Are your hands clean, minion?

CORISCA
Yes, forsooth.

ZANTHIA
Fall off then. She and I have changed our parts;
She does what she forced me to do in her reign,
And I must practise it in mine.

GRACCULO
'Tis justice:
O! here come more.

[Enter **CIMBRIO, CLEON, POLIPHRON**, and **OLYMPIA**.

CIMBRIO
Discover to a drachma,
Or I will famish thee.

CLEON
O! I am pined already.

POLIPHRON
Spare the old jade, he's founder'd.

GRACCULO
Cut his throat then,
And hang him out for a scarecrow.

POLIPHRON
You have all your wishes
In your revenge, and I have mine. You see
I use no tyranny: once I was her slave,
And in requital of her courtesies,
Having made one another free, we are married:
And, if you wish us joy, join with us in
A dance at our wedding.

GRACCULO
Agreed; for I have thought of
A most triumphant one, which shall express
We are lords, and these our slaves.

POLIPHRON
But we shall want
A woman.

GRACCULO
No, here's Jane-of-apes shall serve [4];
Carry your body swimming.—Where's the music?

POLIPHRON
I have placed it in yon window.

GRACCULO
Begin then sprightly.

[Music, and then a dance.

[Enter **MARULLO** behind.

POLIPHRON
Well done on all sides! I have prepared a banquet;
Let's drink and cool us.

GRACCULO
A good motion.

CIMBRIO
Wait here;
You have been tired with feasting, learn to fast now.

GRACCULO
I'll have an apple for jack, and may be some scraps
May fall to your share.

[Exeunt **GRACCULO, ZANTHIA, CIMBRIO, POLIPHRON** and **OLYMPIA**.

CORISCA
Whom can we accuse
But ourselves, for what we suffer? Thou art just,
Thou all-creating Power! and misery
Instructs me now, that yesterday acknowledged
No deity beyond my pride and pleasure,
There is a heaven above us, that looks down
With the eyes of justice, upon such as number
Those blessings freely given, in the accompt
Of their poor merits: else it could not be,
Now miserable I, to please whose palate
The elements were ransack'd, yet complain'd
Of nature, as not liberal enough
In her provision of rarities
To soothe my taste, and pamper my proud flesh,
Should wish in vain for bread.

CLEON
Yes, I do wish too,
For what I fed my dogs with.

CORISCA
I, that forgot
I was made of flesh and blood, and thought the silk
Spun by the diligent worm out of their entrails,
Too coarse to clothe me, and the softest down
Too hard to sleep on; that disdain'd to look
On virtue being in rags, that from my servants
Expected adoration, am made justly
The scorn of my own bondwoman.

CLEON
I know I cannot
Last long, that's all my comfort.

MARULLO
What a true mirror
Were this sad spectacle for secure greatness!
Here they, that never see themselves, but in
The glass of servile flattery, might behold
The weak foundation upon which they build
Their trust in human frailty. Happy are those,
That knowing, in their births, they are subject to
Uncertain change, are still prepared, and arm'd
For either fortune: a rare principle,
And, with much labour, learn'd in wisdom's school!
For, as these bondmen, by their actions, show
That their prosperity, like too large a sail
For their small bark of judgment, sinks them with
A fore-right gale of liberty, ere they reach
The port they long to touch at: so these wretches,
Swollen with the false opinion of their worth,
And proud of blessings left them, not acquired;
That did believe they could with giant arms
Fathom the earth, and were above their fates,
Those borrow'd helps, that did support them, vanish'd,
Fall of themselves, and by unmanly suffering
Betray their proper weakness, and make known
Their boasted greatness was lent, not their own.

CLEON
O for some meat! they sit long.

CORISCA
We forgot,

When we drew out intemperate feasts till midnight;
Their hunger was not thought on, nor their watchings;
Nor did we hold ourselves served to the height,
But when we did exact and force their duties
Beyond their strength and power.

ASOTUS
We pay for 't now:

[Re-enter **POLIPHRON, CIMBRIO, GRACCULO, ZANTHIA**, and **OLYMPIA**, drunk and quarrelling.

CIMBRIO
Do not hold me:
Not kiss the bride!

POLIPHRON
No, sir.

MARULLO [coming forward]
Hold!

ZANTHIA
Here's Marullo.

OLYMPIA
He's your chief.

MARULLO
Take heed; I've news will cool this heat, and make you
Remember what you were.

CIMBRIO
How!

MARULLO
Send off these,
And then I'll tell you.

[Exeunt **CLEON, ASOTUS, ZANTHIA, OLYMPIA** and **CORIS**CA.

CIMBRIO
What would you impart?

MARULLO
What must invite you
To stand upon your guard, and leave your feasting;
Our masters are victorious.

OMNES
How!

MARULLO
Within
A day's march of the city, flesh'd with spoil,
And proud of conquest; the armado sunk,
The Carthaginian admiral, hand to hand,
Slain by Leosthenes.

CIMBRIO
I feel the whip
Upon my back already.

GRACCULO
Every man
Seek a convenient tree, and hang himself.

POLIPHRON
Better die once, than live an age to suffer
New tortures every hour.

CIMBRIO
Say, we submit,
And yield us to their mercy?—

MARULLO
Can you flatter
Yourselves with such false hopes? Or dare you think
That your imperious lords, that never fail'd
To punish with severity petty slips
In your neglect of labour, may be won
To pardon those licentious outrages
Which noble enemies forbear to practise
Upon the conquer'd? We have gone too far
To think now of retiring; in our courage,
And daring, lies our safety: if you are not
Slaves in your abject minds, as in your fortunes,
Since to die is the worst, better expose
Our naked breasts to their keen swords, and sell
Our lives with the most advantage, than to trust
In a forestall'd remission, or yield up
Our bodies to the furnace of their fury,
Thrice heated with revenge.

GRACCULO
You led us on.

CIMBRIO
And 'tis but justice you should bring us off.

GRACCULO
And we expect it.

MARULLO
Hear then, and obey me;
And I will either save you, or fall with you.
Man the walls strongly, and make good the ports;
Boldly deny their entrance, and rip up
Your grievances, and what compell'd you to
This desperate course: if they disdain to hear
Of composition, we have in our powers
Their aged fathers, children, and their wives,
Who, to preserve themselves, must willingly
Make intercession for us. 'Tis not time now
To talk, but do: a glorious end, or freedom,
Is now proposed us; stand resolved for either,
And, like good fellows, live or die together.

[Exeunt.

FOOTNOTES

[1] *Moppes,] i. e. the quick and grinning motions of the teeth and lips which apes make when they are irritated.*

[2] *What for ourself, your lord?] Here Asotus must be supposed to leap, or rather tumble, in token of obedience. Our ancestors certainly excelled us in the education which they bestowed on their animals. Banks's horse far surpassed all that have been brought up in the academy of Mr. Astley; and the apes of these days are mere clowns to their progenitors. The apes of Massinger's time were gifted with a pretty smattering of politics and philosophy. The widow Wild had one of them: "He would come over for all my friends, but was the dogged'st thing to my enemies! He would sit upon his tail before them, and frown like John-a-napes when the pope is named." The Parson's Wedding.—GIFFORD.*

[3] *Let us, like conquering Romans, walk in triumph.] Gracculo speaks in the spirit of prophecy; for the conquering Romans were at this time struggling with their neighbours for a few miserable huts to hide their heads in; and if any captives followed, or rather preceded, their triumphs, it was a herd of stolen beeves.—GIFFORD.*

[4] *Jane-of-apes;] Meaning Corisca: he plays upon Jack-an-apes, the name he had given to Asotus.—GIFFORD.*

SCENE IV

The Country Near Syracuse. The Camp of Timoleon.

Enter **LEOSTHENES** and **TIMAGORAS**.

TIMAGORAS
I am so far from envy, I am proud
You have outstripp'd me in the race of honour.
O 'twas a glorious day, and bravely won!
Your bold performance gave such lustre to
Timoleon's wise directions, as the army
Rests doubtful, to whom they stand most engaged
For their so great success.

LEOSTHENES
The gods first honour'd,
The glory be the general's; 'tis far from me
To be his rival.

TIMAGORAS
You abuse your fortune,
To entertain her choice and gracious favours
With a contracted brow; plumed Victory
Is truly painted with a cheerful look,
Equally distant from proud insolence,
And base dejection.

LEOSTHENES
O Timagoras,
You only are acquainted with the cause
That loads my sad heart with a hill of lead;
Whose ponderous weight, neither my new-got honour,
Assisted by the general applause
The soldier crowns it with, nor all war's glories,
Can lessen or remove: and, would you please,
With fit consideration, to remember
How much I wrong'd Cleora's innocence
With my rash doubts; and what a grievous penance
She did impose upon her tender sweetness,
To pluck away the vulture, jealousy,
That fed upon my liver; you cannot blame me,
But call it a fit justice on myself,
Though I resolve to be a stranger to
The thought of mirth or pleasure.

TIMAGORAS
You have redeem'd
The forfeit of your fault with such a ransom

Of honourable action, as my sister
Must of necessity confess her sufferings,
Weigh'd down by your fair merits; and, when she views you,
Like a triumphant conqueror, carried through
The streets of Syracusa, the glad people
Pressing to meet you, and the senators
Contending who shall heap most honours on you;
The oxen, crown'd with garlands, led before you,
Appointed for the sacrifice; and the altars
Smoking with thankful incense to the gods:
The soldiers chanting loud hymns to your praise,
The windows fill'd with matrons and with virgins,
Throwing upon your head, as you pass by,
The choicest flowers, and silently invoking
The queen of love, with their particular vows,
To be thought worthy of you; can Cleora
(Though, in the glass of self-love, she behold
Her best deserts) but with all joy acknowledge
What she endured was but a noble trial
You made of her affection? and her anger,
Rising from your too amorous cares, soon drench'd
In Lethe, and forgotten.

LEOSTHENES
If those glories
You so set forth were mine, they might plead for me;
But I can lay no claim to the least honour
Which you, with foul injustice, ravish from her.
Her beauty in me wrought a miracle,
Taught me to aim at things beyond my power,
Which her perfections purchased, and gave to me
From her free bounties; she inspired me with
That valour which I dare not call mine own;
And, from the fair reflection of her mind,
My soul received the sparkling beams of courage.
She, from the magazine of her proper goodness,
Stock'd me with virtuous purposes; sent me forth
To trade for honour; and, she being the owner
Of the bark of my adventures, I must yield her
A just account of all, as fits a factor.
And, howsoever others think me happy,
And cry aloud, I have made a prosperous voyage;
One frown of her dislike at my return,
Which, as a punishment for my fault, I look for,
Strikes dead all comfort.

TIMAGORAS
Tush! these fears are needless;

She cannot, must not, shall not, be so cruel.
A free confession of a fault wins pardon,
But, being seconded by desert, commands it.
The general is your own, and, sure, my father
Repents his harshness; for myself, I am
Ever your creature.—One day shall be happy
In your triumph, and your marriage.

LEOSTHENES
May it prove so,
With her consent and pardon.

TIMAGORAS
Ever touching
On that harsh string! She is your own, and you
Without disturbance seize on what's your due.

[Exeunt.

ACT IV

SCENE I

Syracuse. A Room in Archidamus's House.

Enter **MARULLO** and **TIMANDRA**.

MARULLO
She has her health, then?

TIMANDRA
Yes, sir; and as often
As I speak of you, lends attentive ear
To all that I deliver; nor seems tired,
Though I dwell long on the relation of
Your sufferings for her, heaping praise on praise
On the unequall'd temperance, and command
You hold o'er your affections.

MARULLO
To my wish:
Have you acquainted her with the defeature [1]
Of the Carthaginians, and with what honours
Leosthenes comes crown'd home with?

TIMANDRA

With all care.

MARULLO
And how does she receive it?

TIMANDRA
As I guess,
With a seeming kind of joy; but yet appears not
Transported, or proud of his happy fortune.
But when I tell her of the certain ruin
You must encounter with at their arrival
In Syracusa, and that death, with torments,
Must fall upon you, which you yet repent not,
Esteeming it a glorious martyrdom,
And a reward of pure unspotted love,
Preserved in the white robe of innocence,
Though she were in your power; and, still spurr'd on
By powerful love, you rather chose to suffer
The fury of your lord, than that she should
Be grieved or tainted in her reputation—

MARULLO
Pities she my misfortune?

TIMANDRA
She express'd
All signs of sorrow which, her vow observed,
Could witness a grieved heart. At the first hearing,
She fell upon her face, rent her fair hair,
Her hands held up to heaven, and vented sighs,
In which she silently seem'd to complain
Of heaven's injustice.

MARULLO
'Tis enough: wait carefully,
And, on all watch'd occasions, continue
Speech and discourse of me: 'tis time must work her.

TIMANDRA
I'll not be wanting, but still strive to serve you.

[Exit.

[Enter **POLIPHRON**.

MARULLO
Now, Poliphron, the news?

POLIPHRON
The conquering army
Is within ken.

MARULLO
How brook the slaves the object?

POLIPHRON
Cheerfully yet; they do refuse no labour,
And seem to scoff at danger; 'tis your presence
That must confirm them: with a full consent
You are chosen to relate the tyranny
Of our proud masters; and what you subscribe to,
They gladly will allow of, or hold out
To the last man.

MARULLO
I'll instantly among them.
If we prove constant to ourselves, good fortune
Will not, I hope, forsake us.

POLIPHRON
'Tis our best refuge.

[Exeunt.

FOOTNOTE

[1] Defeature,] i. e. defeat. The two words were used indiscriminately by our old writers.

SCENE II

Before the Walls of Syracuse.

Enter **TIMOLEON, ARCHIDAMUS, DIPHILUS, LEOSTHENES, TIMAGORAS,** and **SOLDIERS.**

TIMOLEON
Thus far we are return'd victorious; crown'd
With wreaths triumphant, (famine, blood, and death,
Banish'd your peaceful confines,) and bring home
Security and peace. 'Tis therefore fit
That such as boldly stood the shock of war,
And with the dear expense of sweat and blood
Have purchased honour, should with pleasure reap
The harvest of their toil: and we stand bound,

Out of the first file of the best deservers,
(Though all must be consider'd to their merits,)
To think of you, Leosthenes, that stand,
And worthily, most dear in our esteem,
For your heroic valour.

ARCHIDAMUS
When I look on
The labour of so many men and ages,
This well-built city, not long since design'd
To spoil and rapine, by the favour of
The gods, and you, their ministers, preserved,
I cannot, in my height of joy, but offer
These tears for a glad sacrifice.

DIPHILUS
Sleep the citizens?
Or are they overwhelm'd with the excess
Of comfort that flows to them?

LEOSTHENES
We receive
A silent entertainment.

TIMAGORAS
I long since
Expected that the virgins and the matrons,
The old men striving with their age, the priests,
Carrying the images of their gods before them,
Should have met us with procession.—Ha! the gates
Are shut against us!

ARCHIDAMUS
And, upon the walls,
Arm'd men seem to defy us!

[Enter above, on the Walls, **MARULLO, POLIPHRON, CIMBRIO, GRACCULO,** and other **SLAVES.**

DIPHILUS
I should know
These faces: they are our slaves.

TIMAGORAS
The mystery, rascals!
Open the ports, and play not with an anger
That will consume you.

TIMOLEON

This is above wonder.

ARCHIDAMUS
Our bondmen stand against us!

GRACCULO
Some such things
We were in man's remembrance. The slaves are turn'd
Lords of the town, or so—nay, be not angry:
Perhaps, upon good terms, giving security
You will be quiet men, we may allow you
Some lodgings in our garrets or outhouses:
Your great looks cannot carry it.

CIMBRIO
The truth is,
We have been bold to rifle your rich chests,
Been busy with your wardrobes.

TIMAGORAS
Can we endure this?

LEOSTHENES
O my Cleora!

GRACCULO
A caudle for the gentleman;
He'll die o' the pip else.

TIMAGORAS
Scorn'd too! are you turn'd stone?
Hold parley with our bondmen! force our entrance,
Then, villains, expect—

TIMOLEON
Hold! You wear men's shapes,
And if, like men, you have reason, show a cause
That leads you to this desperate course, which must end
In your destruction.

GRACCULO
That, as please the Fates;
But we vouchsafe—Speak, captain.

TIMAGORAS
Hell and furies!

ARCHIDAMUS

Bay'd by our own curs!

CIMBRIO
Take heed you be not worried.

POLIPHRON
We are sharp set.

CIMBRIO
And sudden.

MARULLO
Briefly thus, then,
Since I must speak for all—Your tyranny
Drew us from our obedience. Happy those times
When lords were styled fathers of families,
And not imperious masters! when they number'd
Their servants almost equal with their sons,
Or one degree beneath them! when their labours
Were cherish'd and rewarded, and a period
Set to their sufferings; when they did not press
Their duties or their wills, beyond the power
And strength of their performance! all things order'd
With such decorum, as [1] wise lawmakers,
From each well-govern'd private house derived
The perfect model of a commonwealth.
Humanity then lodged in the hearts of men,
And thankful masters carefully provided
For creatures wanting reason. The noble horse,
That, in his fiery youth, from his wide nostrils
Neigh'd courage to his rider, and brake through
Groves of opposed pikes, bearing his lord
Safe to triumphant victory; old or wounded,
Was set at liberty, and freed from service.
The Athenian mules, that from the quarry drew
Marble, hew'd for the temples of the gods,
The great work ended, were dismiss'd, and fed
At the public cost; nay, faithful dogs have found
Their sepulchres; but man, to man more cruel,
Appoints no end to the sufferings of his slave;
Since pride stepp'd in and riot, and o'erturn'd
This goodly frame of concord, teaching masters
To glory in the abuse of such as are
Brought under their command; who, grown unuseful,
Are less esteem'd than beasts.—This you have practised,
Practised on us with rigour; this hath forced us
To shake our heavy yokes off; and, if redress
Of these just grievances be not granted us,

We'll right ourselves, and by strong hand defend
What we are now possess'd of.

GRACCULO
And not leave
One house unfired.

CIMBRIO
Or throat uncut of those
We have in our power.

POLIPHRON
Nor will we fall alone;
You shall buy us dearly.

TIMAGORAS
O the gods!
Unheard-of insolence!

TIMOLEON
What are your demands?

MARULLO
A general pardon [2] first, for all offences
Committed in your absence. Liberty
To all such as desire to make return
Into their countries; and, to those that stay,
A competence of land freely allotted
To each man's proper use, no lord acknowledged:
Lastly, with your consent, to choose them wives
Out of your families.

TIMAGORAS
Let the city sink first.

LEOSTHENES
And ruin seize on all, ere we subscribe
To such conditions.

ARCHIDAMUS
Carthage, though victorious,
Could not have forced more from us.

LEOSTHENES
Scale the walls;
Capitulate after.

TIMOLEON

He that wins the top first
Shall wear a mural wreath.

[Exeunt.

MARULLO
Each to his place.

[Flourish and alarms.

Or death or victory! Charge them home, and fear not.

[Exeunt **MARULLO** and **SLAVES**.

[Re-enter **TIMOLEON, ARCHIDAMUS**, and **SENATORS**.

TIMOLEON
We wrong ourselves, and we are justly punish'd,
To deal with bondmen, as if we encounter'd
An equal enemy.

ARCHIDAMUS
They fight like devils;
And run upon our swords, as if their breasts
Were proof beyond their armour.

[Re-enter **LEOSTHENES** and **TIMAGORAS**.

TIMAGORAS
Make a firm stand.
The slaves, not satisfied they have beat us off,
Prepare to sally forth.

TIMOLEON
They are wild beasts,
And to be tamed by policy. Each man take
A tough whip in his hand, such as you used
To punish them with, as masters: in your looks
Carry severity and awe: 'twill fright them
More than your weapons. Savage lions fly from
The sight of fire; and these, that have forgot
That duty you ne'er taught them with your swords,
When, unexpected, they behold those terrors
Advanced aloft, that they were made to shake at,
'Twill force them to remember what they are,
And stoop to due obedience.

ARCHIDAMUS

Here they come.

[Enter from the City, **CIMBRIO**, **GRACCULO**, and other **SLAVES**.

CIMBRIO
Leave not a man alive; a wound's but a flea-biting,
To what we suffer'd, being slaves.

GRACCULO
O, my heart!
Cimbrio, what do we see? the whip! our masters!

TIMAGORAS
Dare you rebel, slaves!

[The **SENATORS** shake their whips, the **SLAVES** throw away their weapons, and run off [3].

CIMBRIO
Mercy! mercy! where
Shall we hide us from their fury?

GRACCULO
Fly, they follow.
O, we shall be tormented!

TIMOLEON
Enter with them,
But yet forbear to kill them: still remember
They are part of your wealth; and being disarm'd,
There is no danger.

ARCHIDAMUS
Let us first deliver
Such as they have in fetters, and at leisure
Determine of their punishment.

LEOSTHENES
Friend, to you
I leave the disposition of what's mine:
I cannot think I am safe without your sister,
She is only worth my thought; and, till I see
What she has suffer'd, I am on the rack,
And Furies my tormentors.

[Exeunt.

FOOTNOTES

[1] *As is, in this passage, an ellipsis of* that, *as usual. Some of the incidents mentioned in this speech, Massinger derived from Plutarch—GIFFORD.*

[2] *Mar. A general pardon, &c.] It is evident, from the unreasonable nature of these demands, that Pisander does not wish them to be accepted. The last article, indeed, has a reference to himself, but he seems desirous of previously trying the fortune of arms. See, however, the next scene, and his defence in the last act.—GIFFORD.*

[3] *Herodotus relates this tale, and Justin repeats it. Massinger may have taken it from Purchas's Pilgrims, a book that formed the delight of our ancestors; and in which it is said, that the Boiards of Noviorogod reduced their slaves, who had seized the town, by the whip, just as the Scythians are said to have done theirs.*

SCENE III

Syracuse. A Room in Archidamus's House.

Enter **MARULLO** and **TIMANDRA**.

MARULLO
I know I am pursued; nor would I fly,
Although the ports were open, and a convoy
Ready to bring me off: the baseness of
These villains, from the pride of all my hopes,
Hath thrown me to the bottomless abyss
Of horror and despair: had they stood firm,
I could have bought Cleora's free consent
With the safety of her father's life, and brother's;
And forced Leosthenes to quit his claim,
And kneel a suitor for me.

TIMANDRA
You must not think
What might have been, but what must now be practised,
And suddenly resolve.

MARULLO
All my poor fortunes
Are at the stake, and I must run the hazard.
Unseen, convey me to Cleora's chamber;
For in her sight, if it were possible,
I would be apprehended: do not inquire
The reason why, but help me.

[Knocking within.

TIMANDRA
Make haste,—one knocks.

[Exit **MARULLO**.

Jove turn all to the best!

[Enter **LEOSTHENES**.

You are welcome, sir.

LEOSTHENES
Thou giv'st it in a heavy tone.

TIMANDRA
Alas! sir,
We have so long fed on the bread of sorrow,
Drinking the bitter water of afflictions,
Made loathsome too by our continued fears,
Comfort 's a stranger to us.

LEOSTHENES
Fears! your sufferings:—[1]
For which I am so overgone with grief,
I dare not ask, without compassionate tears,
The villain's name that robb'd thee of thy honour:
For being train'd up in chastity's cold school,
And taught by such a mistress as Cleora,
'Twere impious in me to think Timandra
Fell with her own consent.

TIMANDRA
How mean you, fell, sir?
I understand you not.

LEOSTHENES
I would thou didst not,
Or that I could not read upon thy face,
In blushing characters, the story of
Libidinous rape: confess it, for you stand not
Accountable for a sin, against whose strength
Your o'ermatch'd innocence could make no resistance;
Under which odds, I know, Cleora fell too,
Heaven's help in vain invoked; the amazed sun
Hiding his face behind a mask of clouds,
Nor daring to look on it! In her sufferings
All sorrow's comprehended: what Timandra,

Or the city, has endured, her loss consider'd,
Deserves not to be named.

TIMANDRA
Pray you, do not bring, sir,
In the chimeras of your jealous fears,
New monsters to affright us.

LEOSTHENES
O, Timandra,
That I had faith enough but to believe thee!
I should receive it with a joy beyond
Assurance of Elysian shades hereafter,
Or all the blessings, in this life, a mother
Could wish her children crown'd with—but I must not
Credit impossibilities; yet I strive
To find out that whose knowledge is a curse,
And ignorance a blessing. Come, discover
What kind of look he had that forced thy lady,
(Thy ravisher I will inquire at leisure),
That when, hereafter, I behold a stranger
But near him in aspect, I may conclude,
Though men and angels should proclaim him honest,
He is a hell bred villain.

TIMANDRA
You are unworthy
To know she is preserved, preserved untainted:
Sorrow, but ill bestow'd, hath only made
A rape upon her comforts in your absence.
Come forth, dear madam.

[Leads in **CLEORA**.

LEOSTHENES
Ha!

[Kneels.

TIMANDRA
Nay, she deserves
The bending of your heart; that, to content you,
Has kept a vow, the breach of which a Vestal,
Though the infringing it had call'd upon her
A living funeral, [2] must of force have shrunk at.
No danger could compel her to dispense with
Her cruel penance, though hot lust came arm'd
To seize upon her; when one look or accent

Might have redeem'd her.

LEOSTHENES
Might! O do not show me
A beam of comfort, and straight take it from me.
The means by which she was freed? speak, O speak quickly;
Each minute of delay 's an age of torment;
O speak, Timandra.

TIMANDRA
Free her from her oath;
Herself can best deliver it.

LEOSTHENES
O blest office!

[Unbinds her eyes.

Never did galley-slave shake off his chains,
Or look'd on his redemption from the oar,
With such true feeling of delight, as now
I find myself possessed of.—Now I behold
True light indeed; for, since these fairest stars,
Cover'd with clouds of your determinate will,
Denied their influence to my optic sense,
The splendour of the sun appear'd to me
But as some little glimpse of his bright beams
Convey'd into a dungeon, to remember [3]
The dark inhabitants there, how much they wanted.
Open these long-shut lips, and strike mine ears
With music more harmonious than the spheres
Yield in their heavenly motions: and if ever
A true submission for a crime acknowledged
May find a gracious hearing, teach your tongue,
In the first sweet articulate sounds it utters,
To sign my wish'd-for pardon.

CLEON
I forgive you.

LEOSTHENES
How greedily I receive this! Stay, best lady,
And let me by degrees ascend the height
Of human happiness! all at once deliver'd,
The torrent of my joys will overwhelm me:—
So! now a little more; and pray excuse me,
If, like a wanton epicure, I desire
The pleasant taste these cates of comfort yield me,

Should not too soon be swallow'd. Have you not,
By your unspotted truth I do conjure you
To answer truly, suffer'd in your honour,
By force, I mean, for in your will I free you,
Since I left Syracusa?

CLEON
I restore
This kiss, so help me goodness! which I borrow'd,
When I last saw you.

LEOSTHENES
Miracle of virtue!
One pause more, I beseech you: I am like
A man whose vital spirits consumed and wasted
With a long and tedious fever, unto whom
Too much of a strong cordial, at once taken,
Brings death, and not restores him. Yet I cannot
Fix here; but must inquire the man to whom
I stand indebted for a benefit,
Which to requite at full, though in this hand
I grasp all sceptres the world's empire bows to,
Would leave me a poor bankrupt. Name him, lady;
If of a mean estate, I'll gladly part with
My utmost fortunes to him; but if noble,
In thankful duty study how to serve him;
Or if of higher rank, erect him altars,
And as a god adore him.

CLEON
If that goodness,
And noble temperance, the queen of virtues,
Bridling rebellious passions, to whose sway,
Such as have conquer'd nations have lived slaves,
Did ever wing great minds to fly to heaven,
He, that preserved mine honour, may hope boldly
To fill a seat among the gods, and shake off
Our frail corruption.

LEOSTHENES
Forward.

CLEON
Or if ever
The Powers above did mask in human shapes,
To teach mortality, not by cold precepts
Forgot as soon as told, but by examples,
To imitate their pureness, and draw near

To their celestial natures, I believe
He's more than man.

LEOSTHENES
You do describe a wonder.

CLEON
Which will increase, when you shall understand
He was a lover.

LEOSTHENES
Not yours, lady?

CLEON
Yes;
Loved me, Leosthenes; nay, more, so doted,
(If e'er affections scorning gross desires
May without wrong be styled so,) that he durst not,
With an immodest syllable or look,
In fear it might take from me, whom he made
The object of his better part, discover
I was the saint he sued to.

LEOSTHENES
A rare temper!

CLEON
I cannot speak it to the worth: all praise
I can bestow upon it will appear
Envious detraction. Not to rack you further,
Yet make the miracle full, though, of all men,
He hated you, Leosthenes, as his rival,
So high yet he prized my content, that, knowing
You were a man I favour'd, he disdain'd not,
Against himself, to serve you.

LEOSTHENES
You conceal still
The owner of these excellencies.

CLEON
'Tis Marullo,
My father's bondman.

LEOSTHENES
Ha, ha, ha!

CLEON

Why do you laugh?

LEOSTHENES
To hear the labouring mountain of your praise
Deliver'd of a mouse.

CLEON
The man deserves not
This scorn, I can assure you.

LEOSTHENES
Do you call
What was his duty, merit?

CLEON
Yes, and place it
As high in my esteem, as all the honours
Descended from your ancestors, or the glory,
Which you may call your own, got in this action,
In which, I must confess, you have done nobly;
And I could add, as I desired, but that
I fear 't would make you proud.

LEOSTHENES
Why, lady, can you
Be won to give allowance, that your slave
Should dare to love you?

CLEON
The immortal gods
Accept the meanest altars, that are raised
By pure devotions; and sometimes prefer
An ounce of frankincense, honey, or milk,
Before whole hecatombs, or Sabæan gums,
Offer'd in ostentation.—Are you sick
Of your old disease? I'll fit you. [Aside.

LEOSTHENES
You seem moved.

CLEON
Zealous, I grant, in the defence of virtue.
Why, good Leosthenes, though I endured
A penance for your sake, above example;
I have not so far sold myself, I take it,
To be at your devotion, but I may
Cherish desert in others, where I find it.
How would you tyrannize, if you stood possess'd of

That which is only yours in expectation,
That now prescribe such hard conditions to me?

LEOSTHENES
One kiss, and I am silenced.

CLEON
I vouchsafe it;
Yet, I must tell you 'tis a favour that
Marullo, when I was his, not mine own,
Durst not presume to ask: no; when the city
Bow'd humbly to licentious violence,
And when I was, of men and gods forsaken,
Deliver'd to his power, he did not press me
To grace him with one look or syllable,
Or urged the dispensation of an oath
Made for your satisfaction:—the poor wretch,
Having related only his own sufferings,
And kiss'd my hand, which I could not deny him,
Defending me from others, never since
Solicited my favours.

LEOSTHENES
Pray you, end:
The story does not please me.

CLEON
Well, take heed
Of doubts and fears;—for know, Leosthenes,
A greater injury cannot be offer'd
To innocent chastity, than unjust suspicion.
I love Marullo's fair mind, not his person;
Let that secure you. And I here command you,
If I have any power in you, to stand
Between him and all punishment, and oppose
His temperance to his folly: if you fail—
No more; I will not threaten.

[Exit.

LEOSTHENES
What a bridge
Of glass I walk upon, over a river
Of certain ruin, mine own weighty fears
Cracking what should support me! and those helps,
Which confidence lends to others, are from me
Ravish'd by doubts, and wilful jealousy.

[Exit.

FOOTNOTES

[1] Leost. Fears! your sufferings:—] The character of Leosthenes is every where preserved with great nicety. His jealous disposition breaks out in this scene with peculiar beauty.—GIFFORD.

[2] Though the infringing it had call'd upon her A living funeral, &c.] The poet alludes to the manner in which the Vestals, who had broken their vow of chastity, were punished. They had literally a living funeral, being plunged alive into a subterraneous cavern, of which the opening was immediately closed upon them, and walled up. The confusion of countries and customs may possibly strike the critical reader; but of this, as I have already observed, our old dramatists were either not aware or not solicitous.—GIFFORD.

[3] To remember,] i. e. to remind, in which sense it frequently occurs in our old writers.

SCENE IV

Another Room in the Same.

Enter **TIMAGORAS, CLEON, ASOTUS, CORISCA**, and **OLYMPIA**.

CLEON
But are you sure we are safe?

TIMAGORAS
You need not fear;
They are all under guard, their fangs pared off:
The wounds their insolence gave you, to be cured
With the balm of your revenge.

ASOTUS
And shall I be
The thing I was born, my lord?

TIMAGORAS
The same wise thing.
'Slight, what a beast they have made thee! Afric never
Produced the like.

ASOTUS
I think so:—nor the land
Where apes and monkeys grow, like crabs and walnuts,
On the same tree. Not all the catalogue
Of conjurers or wise women bound together

Could have so soon transform'd me, as my rascal
Did with his whip; for not in outside only,
But in my own belief, I thought myself
As perfect a baboon—

TIMAGORAS
An ass thou wert ever.

ASOTUS
And would have given one leg, with all my heart,
For good security to have been a man
After three lives, or one and twenty years,
Though I had died on crutches.

CLEON
Never varlets
So triumph'd o'er an old fat man: I was famish'd.

TIMAGORAS
Indeed you are fallen away.

ASOTUS
Three years of feeding
On cullises and jelly, though his cooks
Lard all he eats with marrow, or his doctors
Pour in his mouth restoratives as he sleeps,
Will not recover him.

TIMAGORAS
But your ladyship looks
Sad on the matter, as if you had miss'd
Your ten-crown amber possets, good to smooth
The cutis, as you call it.

CORISCA
Pray you, forbear;
I am an alter'd woman.

TIMAGORAS
So it seems;
A part of your honour's ruff stands out of rank too.

CORISCA
No matter, I have other thoughts.

TIMAGORAS
O strange!
Not ten days since it would have vex'd you more

Than the loss of your good name.

[Enter **LEOSTHENES** and **DIPHILUS** with a **GUARD**.

How now, friend!
Looks our Cleora lovely?

LEOSTHENES
In my thoughts, sir.

TIMAGORAS
But why this guard?

DIPHILUS
It is Timoleon's pleasure:
The slaves have been examined, and confess
Their riot took beginning from your house;
And the first mover of them to rebellion
Your slave Marullo.

[Exeunt **DIPHILUS**. and **GUARD**.

LEOSTHENES
Ha! I more than fear.

TIMAGORAS
They may search boldly.

[Enter **TIMANDRA**, speaking to the **GUARD** within.

TIMANDRA
You are unmanner'd grooms.
To pry into my lady's private lodgings:
There's no Marullos there.

[Re-enter **DIPHILUS**, and **GUARD**, with **MARULLO**.

TIMAGORAS
Now I suspect too.
Where found you him?

DIPHILUS
Close hid in your sister's chamber.

TIMAGORAS
Is that the villain's sanctuary?

LEOSTHENES

This confirms
All she deliver'd, false.

TIMAGORAS
But that I scorn
To rust my good sword in thy slavish blood,
Thou now wert dead.

MARULLO
He's more a slave than fortune
Or misery can make me, that insults
Upon unweapon'd innocence.

TIMAGORAS
Prate you, dog?

MARULLO
Curs snap at lions in the toil, whose looks
Frighted them, being free.

TIMAGORAS
As a wild beast,
Drive him before you.

MARULLO
O divine Cleora!

LEOSTHENES
Darest thou presume to name her?

MARULLO
Yes, and love her;
And may say, have deserved her.

TIMAGORAS
Stop his mouth,
Load him with irons too.

[Exit **GUARD** with **MARULLO**.

CLEON
I am deadly sick
To look on him.

ASOTUS
If he get loose, I know it,
I caper like an ape again: I feel
The whip already.

TIMANDRA
This goes to my lady.

[Exit.

TIMAGORAS
Come, cheer you, sir; we'll urge his punishment
To the full satisfaction of your anger.

LEOSTHENES
He is not worth my thoughts. No corner left
In all the spacious rooms of my vex'd heart,
But is fill'd with Cleora: and the rape
She has done upon her honour, with my wrong,
The heavy burden of my sorrow's song.

[Exeunt.

ACT V

SCENE I

The Same. A Room in Archidamus's House.

Enter **ARCHIDAMUS** and **CLEORA**.

ARCHIDAMUS
Thou art thine own disposer. Were his honours
And glories centupled, as I must confess,
Leosthenes is most worthy, yet I will not,
However I may counsel, force affection.

CLEON
It needs not, sir; I prize him to his worth,
Nay, love him truly; yet would not live slaved
To his jealous humours: since, by the hopes of heaven,
As I am free from violence, in a thought
I am not guilty.

ARCHIDAMUS
'Tis believed, Cleora;
And much the rather, our great gods be praised for 't!
In that I find, beyond my hopes, no sign
Of riot in my house, but all things order'd,
As if I had been present.

CLEON
May that move you
To pity poor Marullo!

ARCHIDAMUS
'Tis my purpose
To do him all the good I can, Cleora;
But this offence, being against the state,
Must have a public trial. In the mean time,
Be careful of yourself, and stand engaged
No further to Leosthenes, than you may
Come off with honour; for, being once his wife,
You are no more your own, nor mine, but must
Resolve to serve, and suffer his commands,
And not dispute them:—ere it be too late,
Consider it duly. I must to the senate.

[Exit.

CLEON
I am much distracted: in Leosthenes
I can find nothing justly to accuse,
But his excess of love, which I have studied
To cure with more than common means; yet still
It grows upon him. And, if I may call
My sufferings merit, I stand bound to think on
Marullo's dangers—though I save his life,
His love is unrewarded:—I confess,
Both have deserved me; yet, of force, must be
Unjust to one; such is my destiny.—

[Enter **TIMANDRA**.

How now! whence flow these tears?

TIMANDRA
I have met, madam,
An object of such cruelty, as would force
A savage to compassion.

CLEON
Speak, what is it?

TIMANDRA
Men pity beasts of rapine, if o'ermatch'd,
Though baited for their pleasure: but these monsters
Upon a man that can make no resistance,

Are senseless in their tyranny. Let it be granted
Marullo is a slave, he's still a man;
A capital offender, yet in justice
Not to be tortured, till the judge pronounce
His punishment.

CLEON
Where is he?

TIMANDRA
Dragg'd to prison
With more than barbarous violence; spurn'd and spit on
By the insulting officers, his hands
Pinion'd behind his back; loaden with fetters:
Yet, with a saint-like patience, he still offers
His face to their rude buffets.

CLEON
O my grieved soul!—
By whose command?

TIMANDRA
It seems, my lord your brother's,
For he's a looker-on: and it takes from
Honour'd Leosthenes to suffer it,
For his respect to you, whose name in vain
The grieved wretch loudly calls on.

CLEON
By Diana,
'Tis base in both; and to their teeth I'll tell them
That I am wrong'd in 't.

[Going forth.

TIMANDRA
What will you do?

CLEON
In person
Visit and comfort him.

TIMANDRA
That will bring fuel
To the jealous fires which burn too hot already
In lord Leosthenes.

CLEON

Let them consume him!
I am mistress of myself. Where cruelty reigns,
There dwells nor love nor honour.

[Exit.

TIMANDRA
So! it works.
Though hitherto I have run a desperate course
To serve my brother's purposes, now 'tis fit

[Enter **LEOSTHENES** and **TIMAGORAS**.

I study mine own ends. They come:—assist me
In these my undertakings, Love's great patron,
As my intents are honest!

LEOSTHENES
'Tis my fault [1]:
Distrust of other springs, Timagoras,
From diffidence in ourselves: but I will strive,
With the assurance of my worth and merits,
To kill this monster, jealousy.

TIMAGORAS
'Tis a guest,
In wisdom, never to be entertain'd
On trivial probabilities; but, when
He does appear in pregnant proofs, not fashion'd
By idle doubts and fears to be received:
They make their own wrongs that are too secure,
As well as such as give them growth and being
From mere imagination. Though I prize
Cleora's honour equal with mine own,
And know what large additions of power
This match brings to our family, I prefer
Our friendship, and your peace of mind, so far
Above my own respects, or hers, that if
She hold not her true value in the test,
'Tis far from my ambition, for her cure,
That you should wound yourself.

TIMANDRA
This argues for me. [Aside.

TIMAGORAS
Why she should be so passionate for a bondman,
Falls not in compass of my understanding,

But for some nearer interest; or he raise
This mutiny, if he loved her, as, you say,
She does confess he did, but to possess
The prize he ventured for, to me's a riddle.

LEOSTHENES
I have answer'd that objection, in my strong
Assurance of her virtue.

TIMAGORAS
'Tis unfit, then,
That I should press it further.

TIMANDRA
Now I must
Make in, or all is lost.

[Rushes forward distractedly.

TIMAGORAS
What would Timandra?

LEOSTHENES
How wild she looks! How is it with thy lady?

TIMAGORAS
Collect thyself, and speak.

TIMANDRA
As you are noble,
Have pity, or love piety.—Oh!

LEOSTHENES
Take breath.

TIMAGORAS
Out with it boldly.

TIMANDRA
O, the best of ladies,
I fear, is gone for ever.

LEOSTHENES
Who, Cleora?

TIMAGORAS
Deliver, how? 'Sdeath, be a man, sir!—Speak.

TIMANDRA
Take it then in as many sighs as words, My lady—

TIMAGORAS
What of her?

TIMANDRA
No sooner heard
Marullo was imprison'd, but she fell
Into a deadly swoon.

TIMAGORAS
But she recover'd:
Say so, or he will sink too. Hold, sir; fie!
This is unmanly.

TIMANDRA
Brought again to life,
But with much labour, she awhile stood silent,
Yet in that interim vented sighs, as if
They labour'd, from the prison of her flesh,
To give her grieved soul freedom. On the sudden,
Transported on the wings of rage and sorrow,
She flew out of the house, and, unattended,
Enter'd the common prison.

LEOSTHENES
This confirms
What but before I fear'd.

TIMANDRA
There you may find her;
And, if you love her as a sister—

TIMAGORAS
Damn her!

TIMANDRA
Or you respect her safety as a lover,
Procure Marullo's liberty.

TIMAGORAS
Impudence
Beyond expression!

TIMANDRA
She'll run mad, else,
Or do some violent act upon herself:

My lord, her father, sensible of her sufferings,
Labours to gain his freedom.

LEOSTHENES
O, the devil!
Has she bewitch'd him too?

TIMAGORAS
I'll hear no more.
Come, sir, we'll follow her; and if no persuasion
Can make her take again her natural form,
Which by some powerful spell she has cast off,
This sword shall disenchant her.

LEOSTHENES
O my heart-strings!

[Exeunt **LEOSTHENES** and **TIMAGORAS**.

TIMANDRA
I knew 't would take. Pardon me, fair Cleora,
Though I appear a traitress; which thou wilt do,
In pity of my woes, when I make known
My lawful claim, and only seek mine own.

[Exit.

FOOTNOTE

[1] *My fault:] i. e. my misfortune. That the word anciently had this meaning could be proved by many examples; e. g.*

Marina. The more my fault,
To scape his hands, where I was like to die."
Pericles, Act IV. sc. iii.

SCENE II

A Prison. Marullo Discovered in Chains.

Enter **CLEORA** and **GAOLER**.

CLEON
There's for your privacy. Stay, unbind his hands.

GAOLER
I dare not, madam.

CLEON
I will buy thy danger:
Take more gold;—do not trouble me with thanks;
I do suppose it done.

[Exit **GAOLER**.

MARULLO
My better angel
Assumes this shape to comfort me, and wisely;
Since, from the choice of all celestial figures,
He could not take a visible form so full
Of glorious sweetness.

[Kneels.

CLEON
Rise. I am flesh and blood,
And do partake thy tortures.

MARULLO
Can it be,
That charity should persuade you to descend
So far from your own height, as to vouchsafe
To look upon my sufferings? How I bless
My fetters now, and stand engaged to fortune
For my captivity—no, my freedom, rather!
For who dare think that place a prison which
You sanctify with your presence? or believe
Sorrow has power to use her sting on him
That is in your compassion arm'd, and made
Impregnable, though tyranny raise at once
All engines to assault him?

CLEON
Indeed virtue,
With which you have made evident proofs that you
Are strongly fortified, cannot fall, though shaken
With the shock of fierce temptations; but still triumphs
In spite of opposition. For myself,
I may endeavour to confirm your goodness,
(A sure retreat, which never will deceive you,)
And with unfeigned tears express my sorrow
For what I cannot help.

MARULLO

Do you weep for me?
O, save that precious balm for nobler uses!
I am unworthy of the smallest drop
Which, in your prodigality of pity,
You throw away on me. Ten of these pearls
Were a large ransom to redeem a kingdom
From a consuming plague, or stop heaven's vengeance,
Call'd down by crying sins, though, at that instant,
In dreadful flashes falling on the roofs
Of bold blasphemers. I am justly punish'd
For my intent of violence to such pureness;
And all the torments flesh is sensible of,
A soft and gentle penance.

CLEON

Which is ended
In this your free confession.

[Enter **LEOSTHENES**, and **TIMAGORAS** behind.

LEOSTHENES

What an object
Have I encounter'd!

TIMAGORAS

I am blasted too:
Yet hear a little further.

MARULLO

Could I expire now,
These white and innocent hands closing my eyes thus,
'Twere not to die, but in a heavenly dream
To be transported, without the help of Charon,
To the Elysian shades. You make me bold;
And, but to wish such happiness, I fear,
May give offence.

CLEON

No; for believe 't, Marullo,
You've won so much upon me, that I know not
That happiness in my gift, but you may challenge.

LEOSTHENES

Are you yet satisfied?

CLEON

Nor can you wish

But what my vows will second, though it were
Your freedom first, and then in me full power
To make a second tender of myself,
And you receive the present. By this kiss,
From me a virgin bounty, I will practise
All arts for your deliverance; and that purchased,
In what concerns your further aims, I speak it,
Do not despair, but hope—

[**TIMAGORAS** and **LEOSTHENES** come forward.

TIMAGORAS
To have the hangman,
When he is married to the cross, in scorn
To say, Gods give you joy!

LEOSTHENES
But look on me,
And be not too indulgent to your folly;
And then, but that grief stops my speech, imagine
What language I should use.

CLEON
Against thyself:
Thy malice cannot reach me.

TIMAGORAS
How?

CLEON
No, brother,
Though you join in the dialogue to accuse me:
What I have done, I'll justify; and these favours,
Which, you presume, will taint me in my honour,
Though jealousy use all her eyes to spy out
One stain in my behaviour, or envy
As many tongues to wound it, shall appear
My best perfections. For, to the world,
I can in my defence allege such reasons,
As my accusers shall stand dumb to hear them;
When in his fetters this man's worth and virtues,
But truly told, shall shame your boasted glories,
Which fortune claims a share in.

TIMAGORAS
The base villain
Shall never live to hear it.

[Draws his sword.

CLEON
Murder! help!
Through me, you shall pass to him.

[Enter **ARCHIDAMUS, DIPHILUS,** and **OFFICERS.**

ARCHIDAMUS
What's the matter?
On whom is your sword drawn? are you a judge?
Or else ambitious of the hangman's office,
Before it be design'd you?—You are bold, too;
Unhand my daughter.

LEOSTHENES
She's my valour's prize.

ARCHIDAMUS
With her consent, not otherwise. You may urge
Your title in the court; if it prove good,
Possess her freely.—Guard him safely off too.

TIMAGORAS
You'll hear me, sir?

ARCHIDAMUS
If you have aught to say,
Deliver it in public; all shall find
A just judge of Timoleon.

DIPHILUS
You must
Of force now use your patience.

[Exeunt all but **TIMAGORAS** and **LEOSTHENES.**

TIMAGORAS
Vengeance rather!
Whirlwinds of rage possess me: you are wrong'd
Beyond a stoic sufferance; yet you stand
As you were rooted.

LEOSTHENES
I feel something here,
That boldly tells me, all the love and service
I pay Cleora is another's due,
And therefore cannot prosper.

TIMAGORAS
Melancholy;
Which now you must not yield to.

LEOSTHENES
'Tis apparent:
In fact your sister's innocent, however
Changed by her violent will.

TIMAGORAS
If you believe so,
Follow the chase still; and in open court
Plead your own interest: we shall find the judge
Our friend, I fear not.

LEOSTHENES
Something I shall say,
But what—

TIMAGORAS
Collect yourself as we walk thither.

[Exeunt.

SCENE III

The Court of Justice.

Enter **TIMOLEON, ARCHIDAMUS, CLEORA**; and **OFFICERS**.

TIMOLEON
'Tis wonderous strange! nor can it fall within
The reach of my belief, a slave should be
The owner of a temperance which this age
Can hardly parallel in freeborn lords,
Or kings proud of their purple.

ARCHIDAMUS
'Tis most true;
And, though at first it did appear a fable,
All circumstances meet to give it credit;
Which works so on me, that I am compell'd
To be a suitor, not to be denied,
He may have equal hearing.

CLEON
Sir, you graced me
With the title of your mistress [1]; but my fortune
Is so far distant from command, that I
Lay by the power you gave me, and plead humbly
For the preserver of my fame and honour.
And pray you, sir, in charity believe,
That, since I had ability of speech,
My tongue has been so much inured to truth,
I know not how to lie.

TIMOLEON
I'll rather doubt
The oracles of the gods, than question what
Your innocence delivers; and, as far
As justice and mine honour can give way,
He shall have favour. Bring him in unbound:

[Exeunt **OFFICERS**.

And though Leosthenes may challenge from me,
For his late worthy service, credit to
All things he can allege in his own cause,
Marullo, so, I think, you call his name,
Shall find I do reserve one ear for him,

[Enter **CLEON, ASOTUS, DIPHILUS, OLYMPIA,** and **CORISCA**.

To let in mercy. Sit, and take your places;
The right of this fair virgin first determined,
Your bondmen shall be censured [2].

CLEON
With all rigour.
We do expect.

CORISCA
Temper'd, I say, with mercy.

[Enter at one door **LEOSTHENES** and **TIMAGORAS**; at the other, **OFFICERS** with **MARULLO**, and
TIMANDRA.

TIMOLEON
Your hand, Leosthenes: I cannot doubt,
You, that have been victorious in the war,
Should, in a combat fought with words, come off
But with assured triumph.

LEOSTHENES
My deserts, sir,
If, without arrogance, I may style them such,
Arm me from doubt and fear.

TIMOLEON
'Tis nobly spoken.
Nor be thou daunted (howsoe'er thy fortune
Has mark'd thee out a slave) to speak thy merits:
For virtue, though in rags, may challenge more
Than vice, set off with all the trim of greatness.

MARULLO
I had rather fall under so just a judge,
Than be acquitted by a man corrupt,
And partial, in his censure.

ARCHIDAMUS
Note his language;
It relishes of better breeding than
His present state dares promise.

TIMOLEON
I observe it.
Place the fair lady in the midst, that both,
Looking with covetous eyes upon the prize
They are to plead for, may, from the fair object,
Teach Hermes eloquence.

LEOSTHENES
Am I fallen so low?
My birth, my honour, and, what 's dearest to me,
My love, and, witness of my love, my service,
So undervalued, that I must contend
With one, where my excess of glory must
Make his o'erthrow a conquest? Shall my fulness
Supply defects in such a thing, that never
Knew any thing but want and emptiness,
Give him a name, and keep it such, from this
Unequal competition? If my pride,
Or any bold assurance of my worth,
Has pluck'd this mountain of disgrace upon me,
I am justly punish'd, and submit; but if
I have been modest, and esteem'd myself
More injured in the tribute of the praise,
Which no desert of mine, prized by self-love,
Ever exacted, may this cause and minute

For ever be forgotten! I dwell long
Upon mine anger, and now turn to you,
Ungrateful fair one; and, since you are such,
'Tis lawful for me to proclaim myself,
And what I have deserved.

CLEON
Neglect and scorn
From me, for this proud vaunt.

LEOSTHENES
You nourish, lady,
Your own dishonour in this harsh reply,
And almost prove what some hold of your sex,
You are all made up of passion: for, if reason
Or judgment could find entertainment with you,
Or that you would distinguish of the objects
You look on, in a true glass, not seduced
By the false light of your too violent will,
I should not need to plead for that which you,
With joy, should offer. Is my high birth a blemish?
Or does my wealth, which all the vain expense
Of women cannot waste, breed loathing in you?
The honours I can call mine own, thought scandals?
Am I deform'd, or, for my father's sins,
Mulcted by nature? If you interpret these
As crimes, 'tis fit I should yield up myself
Most miserably guilty. But, perhaps,
(Which yet I would not credit,) you have seen
This gallant pitch the bar, or bear a burden
Would crack the shoulders of a weaker bondman.

CLEON
You are foul-mouth'd.

ARCHIDAMUS
Ill-manner'd too.

LEOSTHENES
I speak
In the way of supposition, and entreat you,
With all the fervour of a constant lover,
That you would free yourself from these aspersions,
Or any imputation black-tongued slander
Could throw on your unspotted virgin whiteness:
To which there is no easier way, than by
Vouchsafing him your favour; him, to whom,
Next to the general, and the gods and fautors [3],

The country owes her safety.

TIMAGORAS
Are you stupid?
'Slight! leap into his arms, and there ask pardon.—
Oh! you expect your slave's reply; no doubt
We shall have a fine oration: I will teach
My spaniel to howl in sweeter language,
And keep a better method.

ARCHIDAMUS
You forget
The dignity of the place.

DIPHILUS
Silence!

TIMOLEON [to **MARULLO**]
Speak boldly.

MARULLO
'Tis your authority gives me a tongue;
I should be dumb else; and I am secure,
I cannot clothe my thoughts, and just defence,
In such an abject phrase, but 'twill appear
Equal, if not above my low condition.
I need no bombast language, stolen from such
As make nobility from prodigious terms
The hearers understand not; I bring with me
No wealth to boast of, neither can I number
Uncertain fortune's favours with my merits;
I dare not force affection, or presume
To censure her discretion, that looks on me
As a weak man, and not her fancy's idol.
How I have loved, and how much I have suffer'd,
And with what pleasure undergone the burden
Of my ambitious hopes, (in aiming at
The glad possession of a happiness,
The abstract of all goodness in mankind
Can at no part deserve), with my confession
Of mine own wants, is all that can plead for me.
But if that pure desires, not blended with
Foul thoughts, that, like a river, keeps his course,
Retaining still the clearness of the spring
From whence it took beginning, may be thought
Worthy acceptance; then I dare rise up,
And tell this gay man to his teeth, I never
Durst doubt her constancy, that, like a rock,

Beats off temptations, as that mocks the fury
Of the proud waves; nor, from my jealous fears,
Question that goodness to which, as an altar
Of all perfection, he that truly loved
Should rather bring a sacrifice of service,
Than raze it with the engines of suspicion:
Of which, when he can wash an Æthiop white,
Leosthenes may hope to free himself;
But, till then, never.

TIMAGORAS
Bold, presumptuous villain!

MARULLO
I will go further, and make good upon him,
I' the pride of all his honours, birth, and fortunes,
He's more unworthy than myself.

LEOSTHENES
Thou liest.

TIMAGORAS
Confute him with a whip, and, the doubt decided,
Punish him with a halter.

MARULLO
O the gods!
My ribs, though made of brass, cannot contain
My heart, swollen big with rage. The lie!—a whip!—
Let fury then disperse these clouds, in which
I long have march'd disguised;

[Throws off his disguise.]

—that, when they know
Whom they have injured, they may faint with horror
Of my revenge, which, wretched men! expect,
As sure as fate, to suffer.

LEOSTHENES
Ha! Pisander!

TIMAGORAS
'Tis the bold Theban!

ASOTUS
There's no hope for me then:
I thought I should have put in for a share,

And borne Cleora from them both; but now,
This stranger looks so terrible, that I dare not
So much as look on her.

PISANDER
Now as myself,
Thy equal at thy best, Leosthenes.
For you, Timagoras, praise heaven you were born
Cleora's brother; 'tis your safest armour.
But I lose time.—The base lie cast upon me,
I thus return: Thou art a perjured man,
False, and perfidious, and hast made a tender
Of love and service to this lady, when
Thy soul, if thou hast any, can bear witness,
That thou wert not thine own: for proof of this,
Look better on this virgin, and consider,
This Persian shape laid by [4], and she appearing
In a Greekish dress, such as when first you saw her,
If she resemble not Pisander's sister,
One call'd Statilia?

LEOSTHENES
'Tis the same! My guilt
So chokes my spirits, I cannot deny
My falsehood, nor excuse it.

PISANDER
This is she,
To whom thou wert contracted: this the lady,
That, when thou wert my prisoner, fairly taken
In the Spartan war, then, begg'd thy liberty,
And with it gave herself to thee, ungrateful!

STATILA
No more, sir, I entreat you: I perceive
True sorrow in his looks, and a consent
To make me reparation in mine honour;
And then I am most happy.

PISANDER
The wrong done her
Drew me from Thebes, with a full intent to kill thee:
But this fair object met me in my fury,
And quite disarm'd me. Being denied to have her,
By you, my lord Archidamus, and not able
To live far from her; love, the mistress of
All quaint devices, prompted me to treat
With a friend of mine, who, as a pirate, sold me

For a slave to you, my lord, and gave my sister,
As a present, to Cleora.

TIMOLEON
Strange meanders!

PISANDER
There how I bare myself, needs no relation:
But, if so far descending from the height
Of my then flourishing fortunes, to the lowest
Condition of a man, to have means only
To feed my eye with the sight of what I honour'd;
The dangers too I underwent, the sufferings;
The clearness of my interest, may deserve
A noble recompense in your lawful favour;
Now 'tis apparent that Leosthenes
Can claim no interest in you, you may please
To think upon my service.

CLEON
Sir, my want
Of power to satisfy so great a debt
Makes me accuse my fortune; but if that,
Out of the bounty of your mind, you think
A free surrender of myself full payment,
I gladly tender it.

ARCHIDAMUS
With my consent too,
All injuries forgotten.

TIMAGORAS
I will study,
In my future service, to deserve your favour,
And good opinion.

LEOSTHENES
Thus I gladly fee
This advocate to plead for me.

[Kissing **STATILIA**.

PISANDER
You will find me
An easy judge. When I have yielded reasons
Of your bondmen's falling off from their obedience,
Then after, as you please, determine of me.
I found their natures apt to mutiny

From your too cruel usage, and made trial
How far they might be wrought on; to instruct you
To look with more prevention and care
To what they may hereafter undertake
Upon the like occasions. The hurt 's little
They have committed; nor was ever cure,
But with some pain, effected. I confess,
In hope to force a grant of fair Cleora,
I urged them to defend the town against you;
Nor had the terror of your whips, but that
I was preparing for defence elsewhere,
So soon got entrance: In this I am guilty;
Now, as you please, your censure.

TIMOLEON
Bring them in;
And, though you've given me power, I do entreat
Such as have undergone their insolence,
It may not be offensive, though I study
Pity, more than revenge.

CORISCA
'Twill best become you.

CLEON
I must consent.

ASOTUS
For me, I'll find a time
To be revenged hereafter.

TIMOLEON
And now, the war being ended to our wishes,
And such as went the pilgrimage of love,
Happy in full fruition of their hopes,
'Tis lawful, thanks paid to the Powers divine,
To drown our cares in honest mirth and wine.

[Exeunt.

FOOTNOTES

[1] *Cleo. Sir, you graced me*
With the title of your mistress.] This alludes to the request in the first act, that he might be permitted to wear her colours. In those days of gallantry, I mean those of Massinger, not of Timoleon, to wear a lady's colours, that is, a scarf, or a riband, taken from her person, was to become her authorized champion and servant.—GIFFORD.

[2] Censured,] i. e. judged. It may be observed, that our ancestors used censure precisely as we now do judgment: sometimes for a quality of the mind, and sometimes for a judicial determination. —GIFFORD.

[3] The gods and fautors,] in the language of the author means the favouring gods.

[4] This Persian shape laid by,] i. e. the dress of a Persian slave, which Statilia had assumed, with the name of Timandra. Shape is a term borrowed from the tiring-room of the theatres. In the list of dramatis personæ prefixed to The Virgin Martyr, Harpax is said to be, "an evil spirit following Theophilus in the shape (habit) of a secretary."—GIFFORD.

PHILIP MASSINGER – A SHORT BIOGRAPHY

Very few materials exist for a life of Massinger beyond the entries of the Parish Register or the College Books, and a few slender intimations scattered here and there in the dedications to his plays. From these scanty sources the following brief memoir is derived.

Our author was born at Salisbury[1] in the year 1584: he was the son of Arthur Massinger, a gentleman in the service of Henry, the second Earl of Pembroke[2]. We must not suppose, from his being thus attached to the family of a nobleman, that the father of our poet was a person of inferior birth and station. In those days the word servant carried with it no sense of degradation. The great lords and officers of the court numbered inferior nobles among their followers. We read, in Cavendish's Life of Wolsey, that "my Lord Percy, the son and heir of the Earl of Northumberland, attended upon and was servitor to the lord-cardinal[3]:" and from the situation which Arthur Massinger held in the household of so high and influential a person as the Earl of Pembroke, we might be justly led to argue rather favourably than unfavourably of his family and his connexions. "There were," says Mr. Gifford, "many considerations which united to render this state of dependance respectable and even honourable. The secretaries, clerks, and assistants, of various departments, were not then, as now, nominated by the government, but left to the choice of the person who held the employment; and as no particular dwelling was officially set apart for their residence, they were entertained in the house of their principal. That communication, too, between noblemen of power and trust, both of a public and private nature, which is now committed to the post, was in those days managed by confidential servants, who were despatched from one to the other, and even to the sovereign[4];" and, indeed, the father of our poet himself was, we know, in one instance thus employed as the bearer of communications from his patron to Elizabeth. We read in The Sidney Letters[5], "Mr. Massinger is newly come up from the Earl of Pembroke with letters to the queen for his lordship's leave to be away this St. George's Day." This was an errand which would not have been intrusted to the execution of any inconsiderable person: unimportant as the occasion may appear to us, it would not have been regarded in that light by Elizabeth; for no monarch ever exacted from the nobility, and particularly from her officers of state, a more rigid and scrupulous compliance with stated order than this princess.

With regard to the early youth of Massinger, we possess no information whatever. Mr. Gifford supposes that it might have been passed at Wilton, a seat belonging to the Earl of Pembroke, in the neighbourhood of Salisbury; but this mode of disposing of his early years rests on a very improbable conjecture. It may occasionally have happened that the child of a favourite dependant was admitted as the companion of the younger branches of the patron's family, and allowed to receive his education among them; but this was certainly not an ordinary case; and, like Cavendish, a large majority of the great man's servants and dependants "left wife and children, home and family, rest and quietness, only to serve him[6]."—Massinger was most likely educated at the grammar-school of Salisbury, where many distinguished characters have received the rudiments of their education, among whom the elegant and accomplished Addison is to be numbered. But wherever the first years of our poet's life may have been spent, and whatever may have been the nature of his education, we know that at the age of eighteen (May 14, 1602) he was entered at the university of Oxford, and became a commoner of St. Alban's Hall[7].

Massinger resided at Oxford about four years, and then abruptly left it, without taking any degree. The cause of this sudden departure is ascribed by Mr. Gifford to the death of his father, from whom his supplies were derived: but Davies relates a very different story, and asserts that the Earl of Pembroke, who had sent him to the university and maintained him there, withdrew the necessary allowance in consequence of his having misapplied the time demanded for severer studies, in the pursuit of a more attractive but less profitable description of literature. Each opinion is equally ungrounded on the basis of any substantial evidence, and rests almost entirely on the imagination of the biographer: what slight authority there is favours the latter supposition, which, perhaps, on the whole, is most consistent with the known circumstances of the case. Anthony Wood, who was born, lived, and died at Oxford; who spent his time in collecting and recording the gossip which circulated in the university respecting the characters and conduct of its more distinguished sons; and whose evidence, however indifferent it may be, is the best that can be obtained upon the subject, confirms the representation of Davies:— "Massinger," says Wood, "gave his mind more to poetry and romance, for about four years or more, than to logic and philosophy, which he ought to have done, as he was patronised to that end." This passage corroborates the account of Davies so far as to intimate that patronage was afforded to our author, and that cause of dissatisfaction was given to the patron; but it goes no farther: it does not even state to whom the poet was indebted for assistance, nor that the misapplication of his academic hours was at all resented by the friend from whom the assistance was received: but still Wood is very probably correct in his information that other than his paternal funds were depended upon for maintaining Massinger at the university; and if such was the case, there can be no question from whose hands they must have proceeded; while the simple fact of his having been totally neglected, from the time of his father's death, by the whole of the Pembroke family, till after the demise of the earl, carries with it a strong suspicion that some offence was committed on the side of the poet, and tenaciously remembered on the side of the peer. Henry, the second Earl of Pembroke, died (1601) the year before Massinger was admitted at Oxford; and William, the third earl, to whom the father of Massinger continued attached during life, is universally and justly considered one of the brightest ornaments of the courts of Elizabeth and James. He was a man of generous and liberal disposition; the distinguished patron of arts and learning; and a lover of poetry, which he himself cultivated with some degree of success. It is not probable—it is impossible—that such a man should have allowed the highly talented son of an old and faithful servant of his family to be checked in his course of study, and abandoned to maintain, through the early years of life, a single-handed contest with adversity, for the want of that pecuniary aid which he could have yielded and never missed, unless some strong and decided cause of displeasure had existed. Had Massinger been merely forced to leave the university, as Mr. Gifford supposes, because the funds necessary to maintain him there had failed with the life of his father, we impute an act of illiberality to the Earl of Pembroke which is inconsistent with the whole tenor of his life and character. From whatever source the expenses of our author's education were originally defrayed, their suddenly ceasing argues in favour of the account intimated by Wood and detailed by Davies. If his father had, during his life, supported him at the university, there must have been some reason for the earl's not continuing that support when the father of Massinger was no more; and perhaps the most honourable supposition for both parties is that which represents the earl as offended by the bent of our author's studies and pursuits. By adopting this view of the case we are saved from the painful necessity of either assuming, on the one hand, that a nobleman distinguished among the most amiable characters of his age allowed a highly gifted and meritorious young man, a natural dependant of his house, to languish in the want of that countenance and protection on which he had an hereditary claim; or, on the other hand, that Massinger had incurred the displeasure of his natural and hereditary patron by the commission of some more crying offence.

Every, even the slightest, surmise of Mr. Gifford is deserving attention and respect; but I cannot admit the supposition by which he would account for the alienation that subsisted between the Earl of Pembroke and our author. That distinguished critic has inferred, from the religious sentiments contained in The Virgin Martyr, that Massinger was a Roman catholic, and for that cause neglected by the protector of his father. But if the intimations scattered through this play and others should be received as sufficient evidence of the faith of Massinger, we must, on similar evidence—the intimations contained in Measure for Measure, for instance—conclude that the religion of Shakspeare was the same; and then we are cast back upon our old difficulty, and have to explain why William Earl of Pembroke, a celebrated patron of literary men, and of dramatists in particular, scorned to yield his notice to the catholic Massinger, while (to use the expression of Heminge and Condell) he "prosequuted" the catholic Shakspeare and "his works with so much favour[8]?" There are many reasons for believing Shakspeare to have been a member of the church of Rome; and the patronage afforded him by the Earl of Pembroke proves, that that nobleman extended his liberality to men of genius without any regard to distinctions of faith; but, on the other hand, we have no just grounds for assuming that Massinger really did hold the same opinions. The only evidence we have upon this point, that afforded by the general tone of his writings, is of a most vague and superficial description. What, in fact, can be inferred from it? We may from such a source derive very satisfactory information respecting the sentiments which would be favourably received by the audience, but very little respecting those of the author. The truth is, that though the national religion was reformed in its liturgy and articles, the feelings, prejudices, and superstitions of the people were still almost entirely catholic; and Massinger, like any other dramatic author, writing for the amusement of the people, necessarily addressed them in a language they would understand, and with sentiments that accorded with their own. Besides, as a poet, he would never carry his theological distinctions to his literary labours: Voltaire himself is catholic in his tragedies; and Massinger naturally adopted the creed which was most suitable to the purposes of poetry, and afforded the most picturesque ceremonies and romantic situations. I feel inclined, therefore, to dismiss entirely the theory suggested by Mr. Gifford, for these two reasons; first, supposing our author to have been a catholic, we have no reason for condemning the Earl of Pembroke as a bigot and a persecutor, who would close his eyes to the merits of so great an author, because his faith did not tally with his own; and, secondly, we have no sufficient grounds for supposing him to have been a catholic at all. But with regard to all such visionary conjectures, thinking is literally a waste of thought.

Whatever may have been the nature of Massinger's studies at Oxford, it is quite certain, from the general character of his works, that his time could not have been wasted there; and his literary acquirements, at the period of his leaving the university, appear to have been multifarious and extensive. He was about two-and-twenty (1606) when he arrived in London, where, as he more than once observes, he was driven by his necessities, and somewhat inclined, perhaps, by the peculiar bent of his talents, to dedicate himself to the service of the stage.

The theatre, when Massinger first took up his abode in the metropolis, must have presented attractions of all others the most calculated to excite the interest, and inspire the imagination, of a young man of sensibility, taste, and education like our poet. No art ever attained a more rapid maturity than the dramatic art in England. The people had, indeed, been long accustomed to a species of exhibition, called MIRACLES or MYSTERIES, founded on sacred subjects, and performed by the ministers of religion themselves, on the holy festivals, in or near the churches, and designed to instruct the ignorant in the leading facts of sacred history[9]. From the occasional introduction of allegorical characters, such as Faith, Death, Hope, or Sin, into these religious dramas, representations of another kind, called MORALITIES, had by degrees arisen, of which the plots were more artificial, regular, and connected, and which were entirely formed of such personifications: but the first rough draught of a regular tragedy and comedy—Lord Sackville's Gorboduc, and Still's Gammer Gurton's Needle[10]—were not produced till within the latter half of the sixteenth century, and little more than twenty years before the stage acquired its highest splendour in the productions of Shakspeare.

About the end of the sixteenth century, the attention of the public began to be more generally directed to the drama; and it throve most admirably beneath the cheering beams of popular favour. The theatrical performances which in the early part of Elizabeth's reign had been exhibited on temporary stages, erected in such halls or apartments as the actors could procure, or, more generally, in the yards of the larger inns, while the spectators surveyed them from the surrounding windows and galleries, began to find more convenient and permanent habitations. About the year 1569, a regular playhouse, under the appropriate name of The Theatre, was erected. It is supposed to have stood somewhere in Blackfriars; and, three years after the commencement of this establishment, the queen, yielding to her own inclination for such amusements, and disregarding the remonstrances of the Puritans, granted licence and authority to the servants of the Earl of Leicester ("for the recreation of her loving subjects, as for her own solace and pleasure when she should think good to see them") to exercise their occupation throughout the whole realm of England. From this time the number of theatres increased with the increasing demands of the people. Various noblemen had their respective companies of performers, who were associated as their servants, and acted under their protection; and when Massinger left Oxford, and commenced dramatic author, there were no less than seven principal theatres open in the metropolis.

With respect to the interior arrangements, there were very few points of difference between our modern theatres and those of the days of Massinger. The prices of admission, indeed, were considerably cheaper: to the boxes the entrance was a shilling; to the pit and galleries only sixpence. Sixpence also was the price paid for stools upon the stage; and these seats, as we learn from Decker's Gull's Hornbook, were particularly affected by the wits and critics of the time. The conduct of the audience was less restrained by the sense of public decorum, and smoking tobacco, playing at cards, eating and drinking, were generally prevalent among them. The hours of performance were also earlier: the play commencing at one o'clock. During the representation a flag was unfurled at the top of the theatre; and the stage, according to the universal practice of the age, was strewn with rushes; but, in all other respects, the theatres of Elizabeth and James's days seem to have borne a perfect resemblance to our own. They had their pit, where the inferior class of spectators, the groundlings, vented their clamorous censure or approbation; they had their boxes—rooms as they were called—to which the right of exclusive admission was engaged by the night, for the more affluent portion of the audience; and there were again the galleries, or scaffoldings above the boxes, for those who were content to purchase less commodious situations at a cheaper rate. On the stage, in the same manner, the appointments appear to have been nearly of the same description as at present. The curtain divided the audience from the actors, which, at the third sounding, not indeed of the bell, but of the trumpet, was drawn for the commencement of the performance. Malone, in his account of the ancient theatre, supposes that there were no moveable scenes; that a permanent elevation of about nine feet was raised at the back of the stage, from which, in many of the old plays, part of the dialogue was spoken; and that there was a private box on each side this platform. Such an arrangement would have destroyed all theatrical illusion; and it seems extraordinary that any spectators should desire to fix themselves in a station where they could have seen nothing but the backs and trains of the performers; but, as Malone himself acknowledges the spot to have been inconvenient, and that "it is not very easy to ascertain the precise situation where these boxes really were[11]", it may very reasonably be presumed, that they were not placed in the position that the historian of the English stage has supposed. As to the permanent floor, or upper stage, of which he speaks, he may or may not be correct in his statement. All that his quotations upon the subject really establish is, that in the old, as in the modern theatre, when the actor was to speak from a window, or balcony, or the walls of a fortress, the requisite ingenuity was not wanting to contrive a representation of the place. But with regard to the use of painted moveable scenery, it is not possible, from the very circumstances of the case, to believe him correct in his theory. Such a contrivance could not have escaped our ancestors. All the materials were ready to their hands. They had not to invent for themselves, but merely to adapt an old invention to that peculiar purpose; and at a time when every better-furnished apartment was adorned with tapestry; when even the rooms of the commonest taverns were hung with painted cloths; while all the materials were constantly before their eyes, we can hardly believe our forefathers to have been so deficient in ingenuity, as to have missed the simple contrivance of converting the common ornaments of their walls into the decorations of their theatres. But, in fact, the use of scenery was almost co-existent with the introduction of dramatic representations in this country. In the Chester Mysteries (1268), the most ancient and complete collection of the kind which we possess, is found the following stage direction: "Then Noe shall go into the arke with all his familye, his wife excepte. The arke must be boarded round about; and upon the boardes all the beastes and fowles, hereafter rehearsed, must be painted, that their wordes may agree with their pictures[12]." In this passage we have a clear reference to a painted scene. It is not likely that, in the lapse of three centuries, while all other arts were in a state of rapid improvement, and the art of dramatic writing, perhaps, more rapidly and successfully improved than any other, the art of theatrical decoration should have alone stood still. It is not improbable that their scenes were few; and that they were varied, as occasion might require, by the introduction of different pieces of stage furniture. Mr. Gifford, who adheres to the opinions of Malone, says, "A table with a pen and ink thrust in, signified that the stage was a counting-house; if these were withdrawn and two stools put in their place, it was then a tavern[13]." And this might be perfectly satisfactory as long as the business of the play was supposed to be passing within doors; but when it was removed to the open air, such meagre devices would no longer be sufficient to guide the imagination of the audience, and some new method must have been adopted to indicate the place of action. After giving the subject very considerable attention, I cannot help thinking that Steevens was right in rejecting Malone's theory, and concluding that the spectators were, as at the present day, assisted in following the progress of the story by means of painted moveable scenery. This opinion is confirmed by the ancient stage directions. In the folio Shakspeare, 1623, we read "Enter Brutus in his orchard; Enter Timon in the woods; Enter Timon from the cave." In Coriolanus, "Marcius follows them to the gates and is shut in." Innumerable instances of the same kind might be cited to prove that the ancient stage was not so defective in the necessary decorations as some antiquaries of great authority would represent. "It may be added," says Steevens, "that the dialogue of our old dramatists has such perpetual reference to objects supposed visible to the audience, that the want of scenery could not have failed to render many of the descriptions absurd. Banquo examines the outside of Inverness castle with such minuteness, that he distinguishes even the nests which the martens had built under the projecting part of its roof. Romeo, standing in a garden, points to the tops of fruit-trees gilded by the moon. The prologue speaker to the second part of Henry the Fourth expressly shows the spectators 'This worm-eaten hold of ragged stone,' in which Northumberland was lodged. Iachimo takes the most exact inventory of every article in Imogen's bed-chamber, from the silk and silver of which her tapestry was wrought, down to the Cupids that support her andirons. Had not the inside of the apartment, with its proper furniture, been represented, how ridiculous must the action of Iachimo have appeared! He must have stood looking out of the room for the particulars supposed to be visible within it." The works of Massinger would afford innumerable instances of a similar kind to vindicate the opinion which Steevens has asserted on the testimony of Shakspeare alone. But on this subject there is one passage which appears to me quite conclusive. Must not all the humour of the mock play in The Midsummer Night's Dream have been entirely lost, unless the audience before whom it was performed were accustomed to all the embellishments requisite to give effect to a dramatic representation, and could consequently estimate the absurdity of those shallow contrivances and mean substitutes for scenery devised by the ignorance of the clowns[14]?

In only one respect do I perceive any material difference between the mode of representation at the time of Massinger and at present: in his day, the female parts were performed by boys. This custom, which must in many cases have materially injured the illusion of the scene, was in others of considerable advantage: it furnished the stage with a succession of youths, regularly educated for the art, to fill, in every department of the drama, the characters suited to their age. When the lad had become too tall for Juliet, he had acquired the skill, and was most admirably fitted, both in age and appearance, for performing the part which Garrick considered the most difficult on the stage, because it needed "an old head upon young shoulders," the ardent and arduous character of Romeo. When the voice had "the mannish crack," that rendered the youth unfit to appear as the representative of the gentle Imogen, the stage possessed in him the very person that was wanting to do justice to the princely sentiments of Arviragus or Guiderius[15].

Such was the state of the stage when Massinger arrived in the metropolis, and dedicated his talents to its service. He joined a splendid fraternity, for Shakspeare, Jonson, Beaumont, Fletcher, Shirley, were then flourishing at the height of their reputation, and the full vigour of their genius. Massinger came among them no unworthy competitor for such honours and emoluments as the theatre could afford. Of the honours, indeed, he seems to have reaped a very fair and equitable portion; of the emoluments, the harvest was less abundant. In those days, very little pecuniary reward was to be gained by the dramatic poet, unless, as indeed was most frequently the case, he added the profession of the actor to that of the author, and recited the verses which he wrote. The distinguished performers of that time, Alleyn, Burbage, Heminge, Condell, Shakspeare, all appear to have died in independent, if not affluent, circumstances; but the remuneration obtained by the poet was most miserably curtailed. The price given at the theatre for a new play fluctuated between ten and twenty pounds; the copyright, if the piece was printed, might produce from six to ten pounds more; in addition to these sums, the dedication-fee may be reckoned, the usual amount of which was forty shillings. Our author appears to have produced about two or three plays every year. Most of them were successful; but, even with this industry and good fortune, his annual income would rarely have exceeded fifty pounds: and we cannot, therefore, feel surprised at finding him continually speaking of his necessities; or that the only existing document connected with his life should be one that represents him in a state of pecuniary embarrassment.

Among the papers of Dulwich College, the indefatigable Mr. Malone discovered the following letter tripartite, which, coming from persons of such deserved celebrity, cannot fail of interesting the reader.

"To our most loving friend, Mr. Phillip Hinchlow, esquire, these.

"Mr. Hinchlow,

"You understand our unfortunate extremitie, and I doe not thincke you so void of Christianitie but that you would throw so much money into the Thames as wee request now of you, rather than endanger so many innocent lives. You know there is xl. more, at least, to be receaved of you for the play. We desire you to lend us vl. of that, which shall be allowed to you; without which, we cannot be bayled, nor I play any more till this be dispatch'd. It will lose you xxl. ere the end of the next weeke, besides the hindrance of the next new play. Pray, sir, consider our cases with humanity, and now give us cause to acknowledge you our true freind in time of neede. Wee have entreated Mr. Davison to deliver this note, as well to witness your love as our promises, and always acknowledgement to be ever

"Your most thankfull and loving friends,
"NAT. FIELD[16]."

"The money shall be abated out of the money remayns for the play of Mr. Fletcher and ours.
"ROB. DABORNE[17]."

"I have ever found you a true loving friend to mee, and in soe small a suite, it beinge honest, I hope you will not fail us.
"PHILIP MASSINGER."

Indorsed.
"Received by mee, Robert Davison, of Mr. Hinchlow, for the use of Mr. Daboerne, Mr. Feeld, Mr. Messenger, the sum of vl.
"ROB. DAVISON[18]."

The occasion of the distress in which these three distinguished persons were involved it is not possible to fathom. We may imagine a thousand emergencies, either creditable or discreditable to the fame of the writers, with which the letter would perfectly tally; but, on such slight and vague intimations, no ingenuity could determine which was most likely to be correct. But from the document a circumstance is ascertained, which, before its discovery, had been called in question. Sir Aston Cockayne, a friend of Massinger, had asserted in a volume of poems, published in 1658, that our author had written in conjunction with Fletcher; Davies doubted this report, but the above letter establishes the fact beyond the possibility of dispute.

Massinger is known to have produced thirty-seven plays for the stage, a list of which is given at the conclusion of this memoir. Sixteen entire plays and the fragment of another, The Parliament of Love, alone are extant. No less than eleven of his productions, in manuscript, were in possession of Mr. Warburton (Somerset Herald), and destroyed with the rest of that gentleman's invaluable collection by his cook, who, ignorant of their worth, used them as waste paper for the purposes of the kitchen.

The great and various merits of the works of Massinger will be better seen in the following volumes than in any elaborate, critical dissertation. If our author be compared with the other dramatic writers of his age, we cannot long hesitate where to place him. More natural in his characters and more poetical in his diction than Jonson or Cartwright, more elevated and nervous than Fletcher, the only writers who can be supposed to contest his pre-eminence, Massinger ranks immediately under Shakspeare himself. Our poet excels, perhaps, more in the description than in the expression of passion; this may in some measure be ascribed to his attention to the fable: while his scenes are managed with consummate skill, the lighter shades of character and sentiment are lost in the tendency of each part to the catastrophe. The melody, force, and variety of his versification are always remarkable. The prevailing beauties of his productions are dignity and elegance; their predominant fault is want of passion.

Massinger's last play—which is unfortunately lost—The Anchoress of Pausilippo, was acted Jan. 26, 1640, about six weeks before his death, which happened on the 17th of March, 1640. He went to bed in good health, says Langbaine, and was found dead in the morning, in his own house on the Bankside. He was buried in the churchyard of St. Saviour's, and the comedians paid the last sad duty to his name, by attending him to the grave.

It does not appear, though every stone and every fragment of a stone has been carefully examined, that any monument or inscription of any kind marked the place where his dust was deposited. "The memorial of his mortality," says Gifford, "is given with a pathetic brevity, which accords but too well with the obscure and humble passages of his life: March 20, 1639-40, buried Philip Massinger, A STRANGER."

Such is all the information that remains to us of this distinguished poet. But though we are ignorant of every circumstance respecting him but that he lived, wrote, and died, we may yet form some idea of his personal character from the recommendatory poems prefixed to his several plays, in which, as Mr. Gifford justly observes, the language of his panegyrists, though warm, expresses an attachment apparently derived not so much from his talents as his virtues: he is their beloved, much-esteemed, dear, worthy, deserving, honoured, long-known, and long-loved friend. All the writers of his life represent him as a man of singular modesty, gentleness, candour, and affability; nor does it appear that he ever made or found an enemy.

FOOTNOTES:

[1] The register of his birth is not to be found, but all writers of his life agree in naming this city as the place of his nativity; and their account is corroborated by the college entry, which styles him Salisburiensis.

[2] Dedication to The Bondman.

[3] Singer's edition, p. 120.

[4] Introduction to the Works of Massinger, p. xxxviii.

[5] Vol. ii. p. 933.

[6] Life of Wolsey, p. 517.

[7] The entry in the college book styles him "Phillip Massinger, Salisburiensis, generosi filius."

[8] Dedication to the folio edition of Shakspeare.

[9] Indulgences were granted to those who attended the representation of them.

[10] Gorboduc appeared in 1562; Gammer Gurton, in 1566.

[11] Reed's Shakspeare, vol. iii. p. 83, note 3.

[12] Reed's Shakspeare, vol. iii. p. 15.

[13] Gifford's Massinger, vol. i. p. 103.

[14] This question ought to be set at rest, methinks, by the following extract from the Book of Revels, the oldest that exists, in the office of the auditors of the imprest: "Mrs. Dane, the lynnen dealer, for canvass to paynte for houses for the players, and other properties, as monsters, great hollow trees, and such other, twenty dozen ells, 12l."—See Boswell's Shakspeare, vol. iii. p. 364, et seq.

[15] The first woman who appeared in a regular drama, on a public stage, played Desdemona, about the year 1660. Her name is unknown.

[16] Nat. Field. This celebrated actor played female parts. He was the author of two comedies: A Woman's a Weathercock, 1612, and Amends for Ladies, 1618. He also assisted Massinger in The Fatal Dowry.

[17] Robert Daborne was the author of two plays: The Christian turned Turk, 1612, and The poor Man's Comfort, 1655. He was a gentleman of liberal education, master of arts, and in holy orders. It is supposed that he had preferment in Ireland. A sermon by him, preached at Waterford, in 1618, is extant.

[18] Additions to Malone's Hist. Account of Eng. Stage, p. 488.

PHILIP MASSINGER – A CONCISE BIBLIOGRAPHY

As would be expected many works from this time not longer exist either in part or their entirety. Further many playwrights collaborated on plays or revised them for later performances and we have used the latest position known on each of them for the bibliography below..

Solo Plays
The Maid of Honour, tragicomedy (c. 1621; printed 1632)
The Duke of Milan, tragedy (c. 1621–3; printed 1623, 1638)
The Unnatural Combat, tragedy (c. 1621–6; printed 1639)
The Bondman, tragicomedy (licensed 3 December 1623; printed 1624)
The Renegado, tragicomedy (licensed 17 April 1624; printed 1630)
The Parliament of Love, comedy (licensed 3 November 1624; MS)
A New Way to Pay Old Debts, comedy (c. 1625; printed 1632)
The Roman Actor, tragedy (licensed 11 October 1626; printed 1629)
The Great Duke of Florence, tragicomedy (licensed 5 July 1627; printed 1636)
The Picture, tragicomedy (licensed 8 June 1629; printed 1630)
The Emperor of the East, tragicomedy (licensed 11 March 1631; printed 1632)
Believe as You List, tragedy (rejected by the censor in January, but licensed 6 May 1631; MS)

The City Madam, comedy (licensed 25 May 1632; printed 1658)
The Guardian, comedy (licensed 31 October 1633; printed 1655)
The Bashful Lover, tragicomedy (licensed 9 May 1636; printed 1655)

Collaborations with John Fletcher
Sir John van Olden Barnavelt, tragedy (August 1619; MS)
The Little French Lawyer, comedy (c. 1619–23; printed 1647)
A Very Woman, tragicomedy (c. 1619–22; licensed 6 June 1634; printed 1655)
The Custom of the Country, comedy (c. 1619–23; printed 1647)
The Double Marriage, tragedy (c. 1619–23; Printed 1647)
The False One, history (c. 1619–23; printed 1647)
The Prophetess, tragicomedy (licensed 14 May 1622; printed 1647)
The Sea Voyage, comedy (licensed 22 June 1622; printed 1647)
The Spanish Curate, comedy (licensed 24 October 1622; printed 1647)
The Lovers' Progress or The Wandering Lovers, tragicomedy (licensed 6 Dec 1623; rev 1634; printed 1647)
The Elder Brother, comedy (c. 1625; printed 1637).

Collaborations with John Fletcher and Francis Beaumont
Thierry and Theodoret, tragedy (c. 1607?; printed 1621)
The Coxcomb, comedy (1608–10; printed 1647)
Beggars' Bush, comedy (c. 1612–15?; revised 1622?; printed 1647)
Love's Cure, comedy (c. 1612–15?; revised 1625?; printed 1647).

Collaborations with John Fletcher and Nathan Field
The Honest Man's Fortune, tragicomedy (1613; printed 1647)
The Queen of Corinth, tragicomedy (c. 1616–18; printed 1647)
The Knight of Malta, tragicomedy (c. 1619; printed 1647).

Collaborations with Nathan Field
The Fatal Dowry, tragedy (c. 1619, printed 1632); adapted by Nicholas Rowe: The Fair Penitent

Collaborations with John Fletcher, John Ford, and William Rowley, or John Webster
The Fair Maid of the Inn, comedy (licensed 22 January 1626; printed 1647).

Collaborations with John Fletcher, Ben Jonson, and George Chapman

Rollo Duke of Normandy, or The Bloody Brother, tragedy (c. 1616–24; printed 1639).

Collaborations with Thomas Dekker:
The Virgin Martyr, tragedy (licensed 6 October 1620; printed 1622).

Collaborations with Thomas Middleton and William Rowley:
The Old Law, comedy (c. 1615–18; printed 1656).

www.ingramcontent.com/pod-product-compliance
Lightning Source LLC
Chambersburg PA
CBHW060130050426
42448CB00010B/2059